The Art of
Juliana Jewelry

Katerina Musetti

Schiffer Publishing Ltd
4880 Lower Valley Road Atglen, Pennsylvania 19310

Dedication

To the Divine energy from which all things come,
my mother,
Teresa Musetti,
for always encouraging me to pursue my dreams,
my father,
Louis Musetti,
for believing in me,
and my beloved husband,
David Kasel,
for his unwavering support and love,
I dedicate this work.

Copyright © 2008 by Katerina Musetti
Library of Congress Control Number: 2007939780

Designed by John P. Cheek
Cover design by Bruce Waters
Type set in Arrus BT/Aldine 721 BT

ISBN: 978-0-7643-2911-1
Printed in China

Unless otherwise credited, photographs show jewelry in the author's collection.

Schiffer Books are available at special discounts for bulk purchases for sales promotions or premiums. Special editions, including personalized covers, corporate imprints, and excerpts can be created in large quantities for special needs. For more information contact the publisher:

Published by Schiffer Publishing Ltd.
4880 Lower Valley Road
Atglen, PA 19310
Phone: (610) 593-1777; Fax: (610) 593-2002
E-mail: Info@schifferbooks.com

For the largest selection of fine reference books on this and related subjects, please visit our web site at
www.schifferbooks.com
We are always looking for people to write books on new and related subjects. If you have an idea for a book please contact us at the above address.

This book may be purchased from the publisher.
Include $3.95 for shipping.
Please try your bookstore first.
You may write for a free catalog.

In Europe, Schiffer books are distributed by
Bushwood Books
6 Marksbury Ave.
Kew Gardens
Surrey TW9 4JF England
Phone: 44 (0) 20 8392-8585; Fax: 44 (0) 20 8392-9876
E-mail: info@bushwoodbooks.co.uk
Website: www.bushwoodbooks.co.uk
Free postage in the U.K., Europe; air mail at cost.

Acknowledgments

A book of this magnitude can only be brought to fruition through the efforts of a combined synergy of people giving freely of their time and expertise. I have been merely a conductor of their collaborative efforts on behalf of this project.

I am forever grateful to my friend and colleague, Debrah Mowat, for her support, counsel, knowledge, and expertise regarding Juliana jewelry, as well as her outstanding ability to produce such stunning photographs. She has been an invaluable assistant in this ambitious endeavor and her significant contribution to this book is priceless.

Dealer and collector Cleora Craw was most accommodating in entrusting me with items from her beautiful collection for photography, while offering her expertise and knowledge in the field as well. I am especially indebted to Linda Munn and Debra Trent, for not only sharing their fabulous collections but for spending countless hours to capture the essence of Juliana, as witnessed in their outstanding photographs; these women amaze me. Many thanks to Don and Terri Friedman, for submitting excellent photographs from their collection, and to Lynn Compton for sharing her special Juliana pieces with us.

I extend my sincere gratitude and appreciation to my photographer, Richard A. Stoner, for his invaluable skills, incredible eye, and grand talent. Without the collections and photographs from these individuals, this book would not have been possible.

I offer my special personal thanks to my gracious editor, Nancy Schiffer, for her vision, knowledge, expertise, and wisdom. My good friend Sara Jane Lowry came to the rescue by contributing her untiring support and expert proofreading and computer skills. Author Paula Higgins selflessly gave of her valuable time in answering questions and offering guidance and assistance throughout this whole writing process; I am indebted to them both. Matthew Ribarich provided information and insight on costume jewelry repair and restoration, for which I am very grateful. Performing artist Noel McLeary so generously contributed her time and radiant beauty by allowing me to photograph her wearing Juliana pieces from my collection, so that we could include images that show this stunning jewelry being worn. Special thanks goes to Jennifer Gregory and Judy Rae Tubbs for their special talents. While all my contributors and benevolent assistants have my sincere appreciation, many thanks also are extended to the Internet discussion groups that are constantly striving to bring new knowledge to the Juliana community through cyberspace.

Finally I would like to extend my profound gratitude to Frank DeLizza for giving so freely of his invaluable expertise assisting the Juliana community by identifying and confirming authentic Juliana pieces. Mille grazie caro Signore. I not only offer heartfelt thanks, but bow my head in tribute, recognition, and awe, to the incomparable team of William DeLizza and Harold Elster, for creating the Juliana jewelry line, which ultimately has made this book a reality.

Preface

My personal journey with Juliana jewelry began in the 1990s, in Milan, Italy, when my voice teacher, legendary soprano Renata Tebaldi, was wearing a lovely cameo necklace that seemed to dance in the light. I was intrigued by the piece, and when I asked her where it was from, she said "America." Her face lit up as she told me of her collection and fascination with this style of costume jewelry, which she collected throughout her performance career. She explained that this jewelry was worn in opera productions all around the world. I have worn Juliana pieces in performance as well, and as my own collection has grown it is my first choice when completing an ensemble. It takes the place of my fine jewelry as it sparkles like diamonds under the stage lights. Juliana jewelry is the perfect choice for that little bit of "diva" within us all.

Renata Tebaldi with the author, at Tebaldi's residence in Milan, Italy. Private collection.

**RENATA TEBALDI as FLORIA TOSCA
METROPOLITAN OPERA, N.Y.**

Renata Tebaldi as Tosca, wearing early Julana jewelry. Private collection.

Contents

1. Introduction _____ 7

2. The Magic of DeLizza and Elster _____ 10
3. Identifying Juliana Jewelry_____ 12
    Terminology, Design Elements, Materials & Construction _____ 12
4. Bracelets _____ 15
    Bracelet Construction Elements _____ 15
    Clamper Bracelets_____ 19
    Flat-backed Bracelets _____ 21
5. Necklaces _____ 22
    Necklace Construction Elements _____ 22
6. Brooches _____ 29
7. Earrings _____ 33
    Earring Construction Elements _____ 33
8. Juliana Manufacturing Nuances _____ 35
9. Dating Juliana Jewelry _____ 37

Lavish Juliana Jewelry

10. Amazing Art Glass _____ 40
11. Coveted Cameos – Incredible Intaglios _____ 68
12. Dramatic Dangles _____ 82
13. Elaborate Easter Eggs, Painted Flowers and Magnificent Mother Nature ____ 98
14. Fabulous Figurals_____118
15. Mesmerizing Margaritas – Rapturous Rivoli – Wild Watermelon _____146
16. Ravishing Rhinestones _____180
17. Is It A Juliana? _____206
18. A Juliana Mystery...Solved _____208
19. Other Companies For Which DeLizza & Elster Manufactured Jewelry ____210
20. Repair & Restoration _____218
21. Storage & Care _____219

Resources _____220
Glossary_____221
Bibliography _____224

CHAPTER 1
Introduction

Costume jewelry collectors worldwide have been mesmerized with Juliana jewelry long before it's creators were discovered. What a privilege to be able to participate in the celebration of one of the pursuits I love, the modern renaissance of Juliana jewelry. The exquisite gallery of over 450 color photographs will not only excite collectors, but delight and inspire anyone who loves costume jewelry. In building this collection, I hoped to select a diverse group of contributors that would offer images that best represent the full spectrum of these breathtaking masterpieces. Within the pages of this book, you are about to be amazed by the seemingly limitless diversity of these extraordinary designs. These inimitable creations are strong, bold, luminous, and gracious, taking the viewer into an enchanted realm. The images presented make up perhaps the largest collection of Juliana jewelry ever published. It is my pleasure and honor to bring these pieces of American history together in one collection for your viewing.

Juliana jewelry has a mystique all its own. It is a look that is sought after and collected by dealers, private collectors, auction houses, beginning collectors, and those who are simply in love with beautiful costume jewelry. It is bought, sold, traded, upgraded, and brought together to create the ultimate goal of every collector, the complete Juliana parure. The discovery of this amazing line of unsigned costume jewelry is only in its infancy today, commanding prices commensurate with signed costume jewelry and at times rivaling some of the other great designers, such as Elsa Schiaparelli, Miriam Haskell, and Schreiner. Recognized for its bold and extravagant use of rhinestones, combined with rare and mesmerizing art glass stones that seem to explode right before your eyes, this jewelry is highly sought after and coveted. A piece of Juliana jewelry is far more than costume jewelry, it is an object of art.

Fabulous purple Easter egg parure of necklace, five-link bracelet, brooch and earrings. Open back Capri blue and Montana blue navettes, aurora borealis chatons and stippled relief cabochons are highlighted with a touch of fuchsia, blue and purple aurora borealis chatons. Courtesy of Debra Trent. $2,000-2,400.

The esteemed creators accredited for these highly sought after treasures are William DeLizza and Harold Elster. These gentlemen set out with a vision that led to the production of some of the most fabulous and desirable costume jewelry on the market today. Throughout this book, you will witness their grand genius displayed in living color, as chapters unfold that address the history of the company, details on design, materials and construction, as well as traits to look for when purchasing Juliana jewelry.

Value ranges are included that are based on the current market trend with a value margin that reflects both low and high prices. These prices are reflective of the market during the time that this book was compiled. Prices may fluctuate and vary in the future, depending on many contingencies, which are based on demand, desirability, rarity, market location, condition, and quality.

Information is provided on repair and restoration, storage and care, helpful tips on dating Juliana jewelry, as well as mysteries that have been solved in identifying pieces. A sumptuous gallery filled with stunning pieces is followed by another gallery of photos dedicated to companies for which DeLizza and Elster also manufactured jewelry.

As you tour the exhibit, you will experience the magic of Juliana jewelry first-hand, witnessing how materials were combined in dimensional layers of complexity to create compelling rhythmic structures that taunt the eye and mesmerize the mind.

Stunning green watermelon margarita parure of necklace, two brooches and earrings. Open back navettes and glistening aurora borealis refract off of the glorious margaritas as light dances around them. $575-775.

Collection of three beautiful givré demi-parures in fuchsia, sapphire blue and emerald green with raised rosettes, open back navettes and layers of aurora borealis chatons. Courtesy of Debrah Mowat. $195-285 each set.

Beautiful examples are captured in color, revealing rare and unusual art-glass stones, including hand-etched floral glass, camphor glass, delicately hand-painted flowers, stones that resemble Easter eggs with speckled, painted and stippled relief work, and more. A chapter is dedicated to pieces that mimic Mother Nature, echoing the beauty of glowing opals, carnelian, jade, aventurine, turquoise, glossy hematite, pearls, and marble.

Beautiful intaglio and cameo sets grace the pages, as well as pieces with glorious art glass cabochons that resemble hypnotizing cat's eyes; and the most lovely multi-hued tourmaline-like rhinestones that, when refracted by light, reflect a joyful rainbow filled with kaleidoscopic modulations of color, justly called "watermelon stones".

Wonderful collection of whimsical owl brooches in every color imaginable. Courtesy of Debra Trent. $155-225 each.

Over fifty fabulous figural brooches are included that incorporate a knock-out array of rhinestones in the shapes of butterflies, turtles, birds, instruments, and more. Both foiled and un-foiled stones are orchestrated into spectacular color combinations, encrusted with huge pear and oval shaped rhinestones, accented with smaller stones, and finally highlighted once again with layers of glorious aurora borealis chatons. Mesmerizing, haunting, beguiling, fascinating, alluring, and yes — absolutely addicting. Once you witness the splendor of Juliana jewelry, you will be transformed. Let the show begin!

Amazing watermelon parure of large collar necklace, five-link bracelet, brooch and earrings. Cranberry open back navettes, purple chatons interspersed with fuchsia chatons and aurora borealis accents glisten throughout this over-the-top ensemble. Courtesy of Linda Munn. $2,300-3,000.

Beautiful slag glass cameo demi-parure with side-hinge clamper bracelet, pendant brooch and dangle earrings. Courtesy of Debrah Mowat. $475-575.

CHAPTER 2
The Magic of DeLizza and Elster

The DeLizza & Elster Manufacturing Company began operating in 1947 with a showroom on 5th Avenue in New York City. The gurus behind this fantastic line of costume jewelry, that we have come to recognize today as Juliana, were William DeLizza and Harold Elster. Their company produced countless varieties of costume jewelry that included sets, bracelets, brooches, tiaras, earrings in all styles, châtelaines, belts, buckles, and even buttons. They also manufactured and sold to a variety of costume jewelry houses and department stores, with more than 700 customers in the USA and overseas. Pieces were manufactured for important well-known clients, such as Weiss, Celebrity, Gloria, Alice Caviness, Kenneth Jay Lane, Accessocraft, Hobê, Sarah Coventry, Tara, Mimi Di N, Hattie Carnegie, and Kramer, to name a few.

Jewelry was produced with what was known as an open line concept, meaning that anyone could purchase from the line of jewelry that was manufactured for any given season. Companies were able to supply specifications to enhance or alter pieces accordingly. At times, customers requested that the jewelry be signed, and after providing the logo, a signature was soldered into place or cast from a mold. Paper hang-tags were also included as an option, at the request of each company. The jewelry was available for sale in sets, that were displayed with a variety of pieces, or could also be purchased individually to complete a suite or parure.

The intricately colored and multi-dimensional costume jewelry that the DeLizza and Elster Company has become known for today was always produced without a signature. The jewelry was not marked until 1967 and 1968, when the company decided to give it a name and identify it with the black and gold Juliana hang-tag. As jewelry was discovered with examples of the Juliana hang-tag, collectors began addressing the line as "Juliana," which has become the standardized name by which the entire line of Juliana jewelry is popularly known today.

The Juliana style was produced from the beginning, in 1947, though the early pieces were manufactured without the use of aurora borealis rhinestones. Most of the highly sought after Juliana jewelry incorporates aurora borealis rhinestones, which is an important reference point when dating and attributing Juliana jewelry. The aurora borealis rhinestone was not introduced until 1953.

The DeLizza & Elster Manufacturing Company closed its doors in the late 1990s, although Frank DeLizza, the son of William DeLizza, is still producing replicas from some of the company's old designs.

Renata Tebaaldi performing in early Juliana jewelry. Private collection.

Acquiring a piece of Juliana jewelry with the original hang-tag is every collector's dream and an exhilarating experience. It combines the thrill of the hunt with the euphoria of that great find. Pieces that are accompanied with a Juliana hang-tag usually command higher prices, due to their rarity. The elegant Juliana black and gold paper hang-tag is embossed with the lovely Juliana logo in two variations: one hang-tag style reads "Juliana Original," while the other reads "Juliana" with a copyright © symbol. Earrings were sold on white stock cards with the Juliana logo. Bracelets, brooches, and necklaces were sold with the Juliana hang-tag, as viewed on the following examples.

Juliana original hang-tagged brooch and earrings demi-parure with watermelon rivoli and margaritas in purples, pinks and heliotrope with emerald green accents and aurora borealis chatons. Courtesy of Debra Trent. $350-450.

Original Juliana earring card with Easter egg earrings, embossed with "Juliana with a ©" and "Fashion Earrings HAND SET." Courtesy of author.

Original Juliana hang-tag embossed with "Juliana ORIGINAL." Photo submitted by Debra Trent.

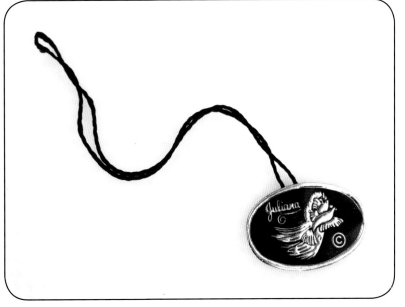

Original Juliana hang-tag embossed with "Juliana with a ©." Photo submitted by Debrah Mowat.

CHAPTER 3
Identifying Juliana Jewelry

Terminology, Design Elements, Materials, and Construction

If American Indians have fifty words to describe the color of the sky, there must be a thousand words to describe the colors and styles of Juliana jewelry. Juliana aficionados have created a unique language that has become standardized in the costume jewelry industry and reflects how this jewelry is defined in the Juliana world. In viewing on-line auction houses and costume jewelry shops, we become familiar with a unique palette of words, such as cat's eye, painted roses, Bermuda blue, sugar beads, rivets, Carmen Miranda dangles, etched flowers, tiger stripes, and Easter eggs. This descriptive terminology has been developed as pieces are discovered within the Juliana community.

Defining DeLizza & Elster (D&E) jewelry and the Juliana style is based on unique characteristics that assist in identifying qualities that are relative to materials, design, and construction. This task is becoming easier due to information that is constantly being uncovered by avid collectors and dealers, online research groups,

and shared by Frank DeLizza. Though many pieces have been identified and verified by Frank DeLizza referencing the DeLizza & Elster design books, enthusiasts are still stumped when a new piece is discovered. Not all Juliana pieces were big, bold, and ultra-glitzy. Delicate pieces were also produced, which makes identification much more challenging.

This chapter focuses on specific design elements and terminology that assist in distinguishing between authentic Juliana designs and those pieces that are poor misrepresentations. It is important to note that DeLizza & Elster used whatever materials were available at any given time in order to fulfill a costumer's request. It must also be noted that some of the traits found in DeLizza & Elster jewelry were also used by the many manufacturers of costume jewelry during this period. In referencing the following guidelines it is imperative that we understand how these elements relate to that jewelry which is classified as DeLizza & Elster Juliana jewelry.

Fabulous Capri blue demi-parure with five-link bracelet, brooch and earrings set with huge pear shaped open back rhinestones encrusted with pointy navettes, lavish aurora borealis dangles and chatons. Courtesy of Debra Trent. $575-675.

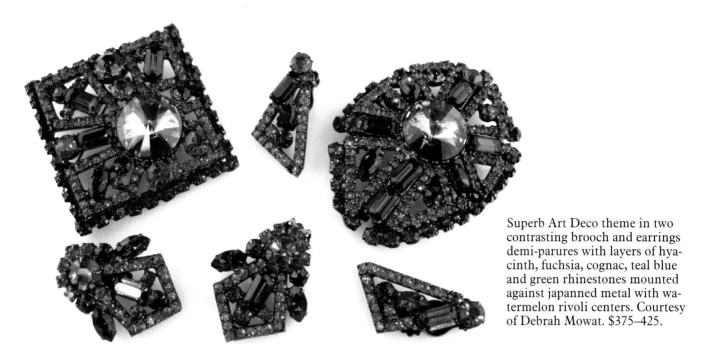

Superb Art Deco theme in two contrasting brooch and earrings demi-parures with layers of hyacinth, fuchsia, cognac, teal blue and green rhinestones mounted against japanned metal with watermelon rivoli centers. Courtesy of Debrah Mowat. $375–425.

Spectacular cascading dangle brooch and earrings demi-parure of emerald green open back marquis rhinestones highlighted with large aurora borealis chatons and hints of emerald green chatons. Courtesy of Cleora Craw. $185-255.

The design elements and construction of DeLizza & Elster Juliana jewelry are formidable. Once you view a piece of this exquisite jewelry and feel its weight and witness the glorious multi-dimensional design structure and sheer brilliance of stones combined with excellent craftsmanship; it becomes easier to recognize and distinguish. Aside from the basic criteria it is important that one uses a hands-on approach as well. By physically examining a piece it becomes easy to recognize all the tell-tale traits that distinguish it from other unsigned costume jewelry. This information is provided as a tool to assist in comprehending key elements that ultimately aid in verification and attribution with focus on the following DeLizza & Elster traits:

• Signature classic five-link construction
• Dimensional layering of stones using a certain type of rivet/eyelet
• Melted mounds of solder within the construction assembly
• Open and closed back rhinestones (foiled and unfoiled)
• Pin-back style and circular ring support
• Findings, finishes and settings
• Tiered and domed construction
• Floating "wire over" rhinestones
• Raised rosettes, brass leaves, filigree and rhinestone balls
• Hand-set rhinestones, prong supports
• Use of rare and unique art glass stones and stones with special effects

CHAPTER 4
Bracelets

Bracelet Construction Elements

The most familiar and sought after DeLizza & Elster bracelet is what has become known as the classic five link construction. These bracelets incorporate five links that are connected with findings that are encrusted with rhinestones, enhancing the design that is mounted onto each link. The links are either rectangular or oval in shape. Most all of the five link bracelets have safety chains, except for the older ones. Three types of findings were used to connect the links. These findings are either stamped with an arrow design, a beaded stripped design, or a lined stripped design that runs vertically along each connecting link. Five link bracelets are an important key in identifying Juliana jewelry and matching up those pieces that coordinate within a theme.

Three five-link bracelets with connecting link examples: beaded striped design, arrow design and lined striped design.

Five-link bracelet with safety chain in large oval open back pale amethyst rhinestones accented with bright purple chatons on connecting links.

The end clasp of DeLizza & Elster bracelets are either bare or at times layered with paste set rhinestones in a lovely horseshoe shape. This clasp most always has an arrow design etched into the finding and sometimes can be found with one rhinestone mounted in the center of the adjoining clasp. A brushed metal closure was also used, but this type of closure is less common.

Close up of end clasp and safety chain on five-link bracelet.

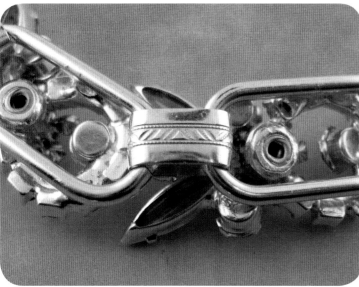

Close up of connecting link on five-link bracelet.

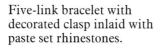
Five-link bracelet with decorated clasp inlaid with paste set rhinestones.

Most stones on the bracelets are hand set with four prongs although multiple prongs and dog tooth prongs were also used. Quite often pieces were constructed with a combination of prong supports as well as paste set rhinestones to achieve a special effect.

Five-link bracelet layered with open back watermelon stones, open back navettes, marquis, fuchsia and aurora borealis chatons with an example of a brushed metal clasp. Photo submitted by Debrah Mowat.

Metal colors varied from silver and gold to japanned and gun metal as well as rhodium and patina finishes. Bracelet designs were often multi-dimensional with rosettes, floating rhinestone wires, dangles and aurora borealis rhinestones layered into the piece to accentuate the special stones used within each creation.

Five-link bracelet mounted with reverse set chartreuse navette rhinestones surrounded by accenting chatons.

Five-link bracelet with tiered construction, raised rosettes and multiple prong support in various sizes of lavender aurora borealis chatons. Photo by Richard A. Stoner.

Five-link bracelet with fabulous chartreuse green keystone open back rhinestones accented with smaller chatons. Photo by Richard A. Stoner.

Example of three five-link bracelets with various mountings displaying smokey gray open-back black diamond rhinestones and aurora borealis chaton highlights.

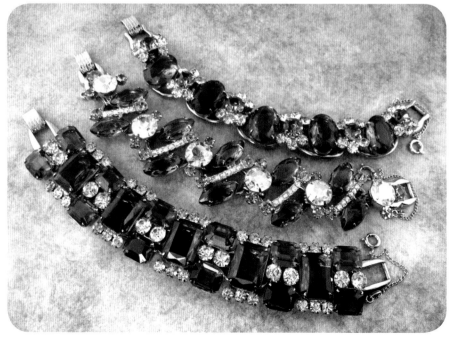

Clamper Bracelets

Juliana clamper bracelets encompass a few design elements that are crucial in determining attribution. One style of clamper bracelet unhinges from the bottom center and closes top center. In referencing the wire used for mounting, it has been noted that only one type of wire was used, being that with the square edges. Those bracelets that are toted as Juliana clamper bracelets and are fabricated with the round wire are not of DeLizza & Elster construction. Clamper bracelets incorporating designs mounted on a wide sheet of metal are also not of DeLizza & Elster construction. DeLizza & Elster clamper style bracelets incorporate a spring hinge that releases when the bracelet is opened and closed. The square wire foundation from the hinged area begins in a narrow form that gradually widens at the bracelet top. This wire continues to curve around the top, trailing back to the hinge.

Close up of interior construction of center hinge clamper bracelet with square wire. Courtesy of Cleora Craw.

Embossed filigree side hinge clamper bracelet with accompanying earrings adorned with a lavish combination of navettes, chatons, margarita and rivoli rhinestones. Photo submitted by Debra Trent.

Close up of interior construction of filigree side hinge clamper bracelet.

Another style of bracelet wire used by DeLizza & Elster is the much coveted embossed filigree design with the side hinge clasp. This style was used in sets with intaglios and cameos as well as those with rivoli and margarita stones, offering various levels of complexity. Lavish rhinestone designs were built up over these hinged clampers that included densely soldered structural support to sustain the weight of the huge stones layered into each creation.

Aerial view of interior construction of filigree side hinge clamper bracelet.

Ghost cameo intaglio gun metal side hinge clamper bracelet demi-parure with embossed etching design and original Juliana hang-tag. Photo by Richard A. Stoner.

Other than the stamped filigree design, a unique and beautiful etching has been discovered which is incorporated into a rarely seen gun metal Ghost Intaglio Cameo clamper bracelet. This particular bracelet provides an example of an embossed etching design that has been stamped into the bracelet wire that resembles etched grids. This style of bracelet also incorporates the side hinge spring clasp.

Ghost cameo intaglio side hinge clamper bracelet interior with detail of etched design. Photo submitted by Debrah Mowat.

20

Flat-backed Bracelets

Aside from the classic five link and clamper style bracelets, elaborate rhinestone encrusted flat backed bracelets were manufactured that secured at the wrist with a box and tongue clasp. These bracelets also incorporate the traditional safety chain.

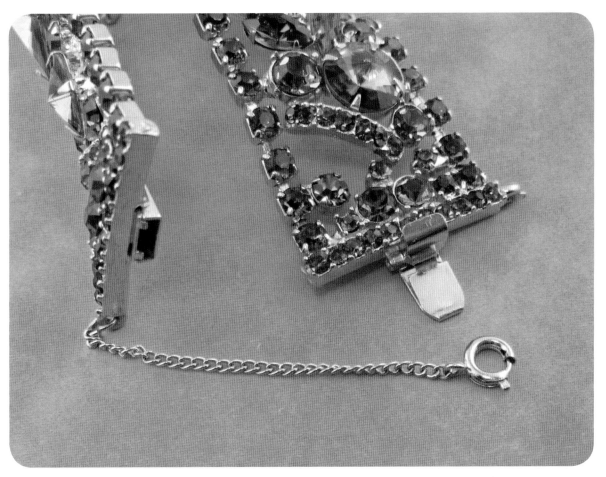

Close up of box and tongue clasp on flat back bracelet with safety chain.

CHAPTER 5
Necklaces

Necklace Construction Elements

Identifying DeLizza & Elster Juliana necklaces is a bit more challenging. The classic five-link construction that is found in the bracelets was incorporated into necklaces as well. You will find a lovely bracelet with five-link construction and a necklace with the same five links that are a complete match to one another. Various necklace designs were also created without the five link construction that include long cascades with dangles, massive collars, extravagant bibs and luxurious pointed "V" shapes usually constructed off a rhinestone chain. Necklaces could either be paired with a five-link bracelet, a clamper style bracelet or a flat backed bracelet. Many times more than one style of bracelet was offered to complete a suite.

Renata Tebaldi performing with a Juliana Cameo necklace. Private collection.

Necklace with five-link construction and floating wire-over rhinestones. Photo submitted by Debra Trent.

Necklace with cascading drops flowing from a watermelon center pendant with original Juliana hang-tag. Photo submitted by Debra Trent.

Extravagant bib style necklace with margaritas and chatons. Photo submitted by Debra Trent.

Necklace with cascading drops layered with chatons and one large rivoli. Courtesy of Cleora Craw.

Front view watermelon necklace ensemble with five-link bracelet, brooch and clip earrings demonstrating the lavish use of extravagant rhinestone combinations incorporated throughout the suite that pull from the necklace. Photo submitted by Debrah Mowat.

In reviewing the back composition of DeLizza & Elster Juliana necklaces, various construction techniques were implemented to attain the support required to build up the multiple layers and levels within each piece. Support structures included ring support construction as well as rivet/eyelet construction, which were swedged into place using gas soldering irons and spools of solder wire. Another construction element was that of an extended bar that was used as a connecting link between the mounted stones (skip chain). This type of support was fragile, but was implemented at times and also used by other companies. Another structural element was the use of a circular filigree finding, which was soldered to the back of a piece for reinforcement.

Back view of watermelon necklace ensemble demonstrating use of open back foiled watermelon stones, navettes and a good example of soldering of components off the rhinestone chain. Photo submitted by Debrah Mowat.

Side view of blue carved roses necklace demonstrating tiered construction. Photo submitted by Debrah Mowat.

Close up of open navette necklace demonstrating extended connecting bar link (skip chain).
Photo submitted by Debrah Mowat

Back view of necklace displaying circular filigree finding.

Most DeLizza & Elster Juliana necklaces close at the back of the neck with a J Hook (sometimes referred to as a shepard's hook) that connects around the rhinestone chain. These hooks are bare, and have never been found with a rhinestone soldered to the finding. The hook may be connected anywhere off the rhinestone chain to achieve the desired length. In heavier necklaces the J Hook has a vertical line etched into it. Other hooks were used on lighter necklaces that were formed without the etched line as well. These hooks were soldered to the end of the rhinestone chain, usually with a rivet/eyelet and are placed on the right side of the necklace. The large bib/collar necklaces use a heavy J Hook that connects to the opposite side of the necklace by going through a soldered loop. This closure was necessary in supporting the substantial weight of these massive rhinestone collars.

Example of Shepard's hook/J hook secured off rhinestone chain. Courtesy of Cleora Craw.

Back view of necklace demonstrating ring support structure. Courtesy of Cleora Craw.

CHAPTER 6
Brooches

Brooch Construction Elements

Brooches were constructed with what is referred to as a built-in pin assembly known as a joint and catch. This pin assembly is soldered into place as part of the complete construction of the piece. At times circular ring assemblies were incorporated into the overall structure for added support and strength. These circular assemblies have been found with a smooth surface as well as what looks like a coiled wire wrapping around the circle. Many brooches also incorporated a bail that was soldered on the inside top of the brooch above the pin assembly. This would allow one to wear the piece either as a brooch or necklace suspended from a chain. This particular chain is what has become known as a Grandfather's chain. On occasion, bar-pins were used for the sake of practicality, though this type of construction was rarely implemented as the company felt that it lessened the quality of a piece.

Back view of domed brooch with built-in joint and catch pin assembly. Photo submitted by Debrah Mowat.

Back view of brooch with circular ring support assembly with smooth surface. Photo submitted by Debrah Mowat.

Back view of brooch with circular ring support assembly with coiled wire. Photo submitted by Debrah Mowat.

Back view of brooch with bail soldered above pin assembly.

In creating tiered and domed brooches multiple sections were joined (swedged) together to support the large structures and stones used within each design. Brooches were produced in multi-dimensional layers displaying various levels of complexity. It is not uncommon to find as many as five and six unique brooch designs to complement a complete suite. Many of the brooches were cast from a design mold which involved pouring melted metal into a permanent or disposable mold that ultimately created the desired structure. Brooches were then elaborately set with fantastic art glass and specialty stones highlighted with open and closed back rhinestone and pointy navettes with a final layering of glistening aurora borealis rhinestones.

Back view of three brooches demonstrating ruffled edge mounting, built in pin assembly, open backs, swedging and rivet/eyelet construction elements. Courtesy of Cleora Craw.

Back view of two brooches demonstrating cast mounting, melted mounds of solder, joint and catch pin back and rivet/eyelet construction elements. Courtesy of Cleora Craw.

Side view of domed brooch. Photo submitted by Debrah Mowat.

Example of multi-dimensional brooch with tiered construction and cascading drops. Photo submitted by Debrah Mowat.

To add yet another element of dimension, a floating wire (wire-over) was soldered to the back of a design that wrapped from behind the piece curving to the front. These wires were accented with a single rhinestone, a miniature flower rhinestone, or a small cluster of rhinestones. Suspended floating wires were used in necklaces, bracelets, earrings and many of the gorgeous floral brooches and whimsical figural brooches. This type of wire was also used by other manufactures and is not exclusive to DeLizza & Elster Juliana jewelry.

Back view of turtle figural brooch demonstrating construction assembly with good example of floating wire (wire-over). Photo submitted by Debrah Mowat.

Front view of brooch with floating wire (wire-over). Photo submitted by Debrah Mowat.

Back view of brooch with floating wire (wire-over). Photo submitted by Debrah Mowat.

CHAPTER 7
Earrings

Earring Construction Elements

Earrings were manufactured in a variety of diverse styles that once again tied into the theme of the complete design. Different choices were offered from simple to elaborate which included dangles and cascading drops in as many as four and five unique designs. Earring backs were most commonly constructed with a scalloped edge clip with three punched holes, though clips with one and two punched holes were also used.

Front view of diverse styles of clip earrings including dangles and drops with both open and closed back rhinestones as well as lavish art glass mounted stones. Photo submitted by Debrah Mowat.

Back view of diverse styles of clip earrings. Photo submitted by Debrah Mowat.

Hard drilled rivets/eyelets were used as part of the base for support in building the multi-dimensional layers. One of the clip components incorporated on dangle earrings is a rivet/eyelet that is soldered off of the clip with an integrated hole that is then used to suspend the dangle. Again, stones were either foiled, un-foiled or a combination of both.

Close up of dangle earring displaying floating wire-over gilded gold etched leaves.

CHAPTER 8
Juliana Manufacturing Nuances

As we study a piece of DeLizza & Elster Juliana jewelry we may notice a few idiosyncrasies that some people address as "flaws". These nuances are a bit of history in the making and an element of surprise that do not detract from the jewelry in any way. These characteristics simply add to the beauty of Juliana jewelry. A bit of balance thrown off center in the soldering of a chaton, a touch of cream colored paper lodged between a few prongs and a rhinestone or two mounted upside down. Many of these elements are used as tools in identifying pieces as well. Each tiny nuance offers a touch of character that not only establishes it as another unique trait and element of Juliana jewelry, but a work of art in itself, "creative serendipity."

This particular style of necklace is found with two aurora borealis rhinestones soldered on two of the open back navettes on each side of the center pendant. This necklace came from the factory without those stones. Photo by Richard A. Stoner.

Side view of necklace. One can see that rhinestones were never soldered into place on the side navettes.

Close up of side view of necklace.

CHAPTER 9
Dating Juliana Jewelry

Collectors are frequently interested in determining the year in which a piece was manufactured. This process is incredibly difficult as we have no patents or jewelry advertisements to refer to regarding DeLizza & Elster Juliana jewelry. In my personal experience I have been quite fortunate to receive pieces that have been accompanied with boxes, notes or cards that are dated. For example, when my Juliana Sunburst parure was purchased it was sold with the original box it had been stored in over the years. What a fantastic discovery it was to find the words "From Jackie, Xmas 1962" written on the inside of the box lid. This tells me that this set was most likely given as a Christmas gift in 1962. I feel I can safely establish that the Sunburst suite was introduced for the 1962 Christmas season, thus dating this suite to 1962.

When purchasing Juliana jewelry always ask that pieces be sent in the original storage box. Also, I have on more than one occasion been very pleasingly surprised, when I lifted the cotton up out of a box to find a wonderful "Juliana hang-tag." Ask about provenance and ask that all original materials be kept with your purchase, nothing short of boxes, notes, cotton and bags.

Montana blue Sunburst parure in original gift box with inscription "From Jackie, Xmas 1962." Photo by Richard A. Stoner.

Lavish Juliana Jewelry

The exquisite jewelry displayed throughout this section offers fantastic examples of what transpires when a true artist's eye is the visual element behind the final outcome. These pieces are all works of art with many of the compositions being fluid, sculptural and multi-dimensional. The essence of these designs seems to create a constantly shifting resonance of joy, intrigue and beauty. Minute details such as gold paint applied by hand to frame the face of a lovely cameo, or layers of colors hand painted into beautiful roses are what make this jewelry so unique, so magical, and so desirable.

CHAPTER 10
Amazing Art Glass

Striking brooch of aurora borealis rhinestones surrounded by purple foiled navettes interspersed with open back amethyst chatons. Courtesy of Cleora Craw. $70–90.

Fabulous tiger eye parure consisting of necklace, five-link bracelet, brooch and clip earrings. Golden amber open back navettes are surrounded by Colorado topaz rhinestones blended with a flocking of Aurora Borealis chatons. Courtesy of Linda Munn. $1400-1700.

Deep sapphire blue givré marbled art glass stone demi-parure of tiered brooch and clip earrings with open back Capri blue navettes and layers of aurora borealis chatons with raised rosette accents. Courtesy of Debrah Mowat. $200- 300.

Exquisite cat's eye parure in ruby red consisting of necklace, five-link bracelet and clip earrings. Fantastic cat's eye art glass cabochons are filled with volcanic embers in hues of gold, red, orange, fuchsia and heliotrope. Courtesy of Linda Munn. $900-1200.

Lovely gold frosted camphor glass demi-parure with tiered brooch and clip earrings. Layers of aurora borealis chatons are mixed with gold chatons that match the center accent chaton on each etched camphor glass stone. Courtesy of Debrah Mowat. $300-375.

Decorated art glass beads in black with fuchsia polka dots are the focal point of this lovely tiered brooch and clip earrings demi-parure. Author's collection. Photo by Richard A. Stoner. $125-175.

Cobalt blue etched flowers multi-dimensional tiered brooch and clip earrings demi-parure with aurora borealis chatons and raised rosette accents. Courtesy of Debrah Mowat. $275-325.

Exquisite butterscotch givré art glass necklace, brooch and dangle earrings parure with Juliana hang-tag. Striking hyacinth chatons dance throughout the ensemble accenting the topaz chatons, navettes and delicate pale green marquis. Courtesy of Debrah Mowat. $800-900.

Lovely japanned fuchsia givré marbled art glass brooch with raised rosette accents, amethyst chatons and open back navettes. Courtesy of Debra Trent. $75-95.

Juliana hang-tagged demi-parure of beautiful gold fluss infused art glass stones complemented by kelly green chatons that are paste set in a lovely horseshoe design throughout the five-link bracelet and matching clip earrings. Author's collection. Photo by Richard A. Stoner. $225-275.

Iridescent carved roses domed brooch with amethyst chatons, fuchsia open back navettes and aurora borealis accents. Courtesy of Debrah Mowat. $255-350.

Beautiful floral brooch decorated with art glass beads in black with fuchsia polka dots and matching clip earrings. Courtesy of Debrah Mowat. $175-225.

Intense cobalt blue givré earrings and necklace demi-parure with a fantastic example of a cascading center drop pendant. Blue aurora borealis chatons dance through layers of cobalt blue open back navettes and pale blue marquis rhinestones. Courtesy of Debra Trent. $450-550.

Elegant iridescent art glass flowers with hints of heliotrope and fuchsia chatons laced with pale pink open back marquis set off the theme in this lovely tiered brooch ensemble with two diverse styles of earrings. Courtesy of Cleora Craw. $300-375.

Mesmerizing Saphiret art glass five-link bracelet, domed brooch and clip earrings demi-parure. This rare special effect stone is infused with minute quantities of gold melted into intense blue stones throwing off haunting pink and pale blue highlights. The stones switch from blue to gold with each movement. Courtesy of Linda Munn. $700-800.

Two exquisite carved roses brooches in diverse styles layered with topaz navettes and accented with hyacinth and aurora borealis chatons. Courtesy of Debrah Mowat. $150-225 each.

Ice blue frosted camphor glass demi-parure with tiered brooch and clip earrings. Note the swirled blue art glass stones surrounded by teal blue aurora borealis navettes. Author's collection. Photo by Richard A. Stoner. $165-225.

Emerald green etched flowers necklace, five-link bracelet, multi dimensional tiered brooch and clip earrings parure. This particular ensemble displays hyacinth accent chatons. This set was also made with green accent chatons, as displayed in the following pages. Courtesy of Debrah Mowat. $850-1200.

Beautiful faux turquoise brooch and clip earrings demi-parure with lovely detailed art glass stones in a floral theme. Intricate variations in metalwork prevail throughout the set with added accents of rose chatons. Courtesy of Terri Friedman, photo by Don Friedman. $145-175.

Wonderful emerald green cat's eye five-link bracelet, clip earrings and brooch demi-parure. Note the lovely brooch design in this set and the intense hues of cobalt blue, canary yellow, Madeira, fuchsia and orange veining throughout the art glass cabochons. Courtesy of Debra Trent. $475-550.

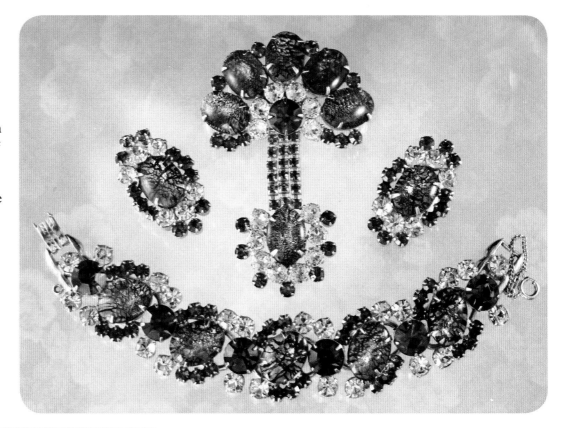

Iridescent art glass flowers are the central theme in this demure japanned demi-parure with deep amber open back navettes and forest green leaves. The brooch is accented with a suspended wire-over flower off the stem while each art glass flower holds a tiny hyacinth chaton. Author's collection. Photo by Richard A. Stoner. $135-165.

Excellent close-up of tiger striped art glass stones are displayed throughout this tiered brooch and clip earrings demi-parure with hints of aurora borealis chatons and topaz open back navettes. Courtesy of Debrah Mowat. $225-300.

Elegant emerald green japanned givré brooch and earrings demi-parure with dimensional layering of emerald green navettes, peridot chatons and raised rosette accents. Author's collection. $150-185.

Emerald green givré brooch and earrings demi-parure with layers of aurora borealis and green chatons, open back emerald green navettes and lovely raised rosette earring accents. Courtesy of Debrah Mowat. $200-275.

Intense gold leaf infused art glass cabochons are the center of attention in this glorious multi-dimensional brooch that resembles the Venetian glass that adorns La Fenice Opera House in Venice. Courtesy of Debrah Mowat. $135-165.

Iridescent glacier-like rock crystal art glass cabochons with every color imaginable from jonquil, topaz, ice blue, fuchsia, peridot and lavendar make up this mesmerizing five-link bracelet, brooch and dangle earrings demi-parure. Accents of green and pink chatons with a touch of aurora borealis bring this set to life. Courtesy of Debra Trent. $525-575.

Luscious and rare carved roses parure with domed brooch, five-link bracelet, clip earrings and necklace with suspended dangle accents. Intense colors of cobalt blue and pale teal chatons gently refract off the iridescent glow that pulls you into each lovely rose. Courtesy of Debrah Mowat. $1100-1500.

Gorgeous olivine givré five-link bracelet, dimensional brooch and clip earrings demi-parure. Accents of open back olivine navettes with layers of aurora borealis, emerald green, peridot and hints of tourmaline green chatons make this ensemble absolutely stunning. Courtesy of Debra Trent. $575-675.

Bold colors of heliotrope, emerald green, burgundy and teal blue adorn this wonderful multi dimensional brooch encased with carved leaf art glass cabochons. Courtesy of Debrah Mowat. $125-175.

Iridescent carnival glass, five-link bracelet with etched glass cabochons in a swirled pin-wheel design. Aurora borealis chatons intensify the warm hues refracted off the rare and wonderful art glass stones. Author's collection. Photo by Richard A. Stoner. $150-200.

Rich olive givré cabochons are layered throughout this lovely tiered brooch and clip earrings suite. Large open back navettes in emerald green are accented with aurora borealis chatons and touches of peridot and teal rhinestones. Courtesy of Debrah Mowat. $175-250.

Deep Capri blue gold foiled art glass necklace, five-link bracelet, brooch and clip earrings parure. Heavy gold foil encrusted cabochons send you right into the heart of the galaxy with mesmerizing rhinestones in accenting colors of Colorado topaz, Montana blue, ice blue and navy blue. Center necklace pendant is dressed with a lovely floating wire flower. Courtesy of Linda Munn. $1850-2250.

Gorgeous multi layered honey givré brooch with cascading dangles of aurora borealis chatons with Colorado Topaz open back navettes touched with heliotrope rhinestone accents. Author's collection. $165-195.

Iridescent poured glass cabochon necklace and earrings demi-parure with a beautiful star and floral design impressed into the glass. Lovely accents of claw set aurora borealis rhinestones in lavender, fuchsia and Colorado topaz set off the glow within these lovely cabochons from Germany. Courtesy of Debrah Mowat. $350-450.

Warm butterscotch givré domed brooch with Colorado topaz and heliotrope rhinestone accents. Photo by Richard A. Stoner. $85-125.

Beautiful collection of four carved roses brooches in varying designs and colors from Capri blue to Colorado topaz. Courtesy of Debrah Mowat. $200-375 each.

Elaborate Bermuda blue givré five-link bracelet, tiered brooch and clip earrings demi-parure. Note the rhinestone rosette accents coupled with ice blue and aurora borealis rhinestones. Author's collection. Photo by Richard A. Stoner. $325-375.

Brilliant emerald green foiled art glass parure with necklace, two pair of earrings and five-link bracelet. Intense gold and copper encrusted cabochons explode with deep green, black and ice crystal veining accented with olivine, emerald green, Colorado topaz and hyacinth rhinestones. The center pendant displays a beautiful floating wire-over flower. Courtesy of Debra Trent. $1875-2300.

Volcanic crackle glass tiered brooch with layers of burnt Madeira and Colorado topaz rhinestones make for one magnificent piece of art. Courtesy of Debrah Mowat. $225.

Amazing cat's eye parure with five-link bracelet, domed brooch, clip earrings and dangle earrings all layered with emerald green and peridot rhinestones. Deep electric blue, heliotrope, burgundy, hyacinth and canary yellow veining explode throughout each art glass stone. Author's collection. Photo by Richard A. Stoner. $525-600.

Electric blue japanned givré demi-parure with raised rosettes, Bermuda blue navettes, teal blue chatons and aurora borealis rhinestones. Courtesy of Debrah Mowat. $165-185.

Emerald green etched flower five-link bracelet, necklace and clip earrings parure. Hand painted flowers are each accented with one hyacinth chaton. The earrings are graced with a raised rosette that compliments the peridot, emerald green and aurora borealis rhinestones cascading throughout the ensemble. Note the larger chatons in this set are green. Another version is accented with hyacinth chatons. Author's collection. $800-925.

Ruby red etched flower dangle brooch and clip earrings demi-parure highlighted with aurora borealis chatons and open back red navettes. Gold paint is hand applied to accent each etched flower which is finally accented with a single hyacinth chaton. Courtesy of Debrah Mowat. $275-350.

Deep amber givré stones are complemented by open back amber navettes, Colorado topaz, warm honey and aurora borealis chatons in this exquisite grand parure with two brooches, five-link bracelet, pendant necklace and clip earrings. Courtesy of Debra Trent. $1200-1400.

Fantastic demi-parure of multi-colored foiled art glass stones surrounded by aurora borealis rhinestones with touches of Montana blue chatons. The intense colors within these stones are remarkable. Courtesy of Cleora Craw. $225-300.

Below:
Mesmerizing cat's eye dangle brooch with accenting rhinestones that perfectly capture the true vivid veining of colors dispersed throughout the glorious art glass stones. Courtesy of Debra Trent. $225-255.

Lovely peridot pressed glass brooch and earrings demi-parure with a pattern reminiscent of the Art Deco period. Author's collection. Photo by Richard A. Stoner. $95-125.

Delicate art glass brooch and dangle earrings demi-parure of a courting couple. The scene on each cabochon is created from a hand applied decal. Touches of peridot chatons highlight the theme within the cabochons. Author's collection. $75-125.

Fire filled brooch and clip earrings demi-parure of gold infused cabochons with highlights of burnt umber, Madeira and Colorado Topaz rhinestones mimicking the colors in the art glass. Note the floating wire over flower off the side of the brooch adding yet another element of surprise. Courtesy of Debra Trent. $325-375.

Exquisite sapphire blue etched flowers grand parure of necklace, five-link bracelet, tiered brooch and two styles of earrings. Note the intense fuchsia chatons accenting each glorious cabochon. Courtesy of Debrah Mowat. $1300-1500.

Beautiful brooch and earrings demi-parure incorporating translucent wedding cake art glass stones with articulated gold beaded accents. Aurora borealis Colorado topaz chatons are highlighted with faux moonstone rhinestones. Courtesy of Terri Friedman, photo by Don Friedman. $85-125.

Rich honey amber etched flower grand parure with necklace, two brooches and two sets of clip earrings. This rare and unique ensemble is graced with Colorado topaz navettes and clear chatons accenting each lovely etched flower. Courtesy of Debrah Mowat. $850-950.

Elaborate watermelon etched leaf tiered brooch encrusted with burnt Madeira rhinestones resting below a layer of hyacinth and Colorado topaz chatons blended with Siam red marquis and rhinestone rosette accents with peridot centers. Courtesy of Cleora Craw. $175-225.

Glorious fuchsia givré demi-parure of multi dimensional tiered brooch and clip earrings surrounded by raised rosettes, open back navettes and aurora borealis chatons. Courtesy of Debrah Mowat. $250-325.

Sapphire blue givré tiered brooch
with open navettes, raised rosettes
and paste set aurora borealis chatons.
Courtesy of Debra Trent. $95-125.

Etched pink art glass clamper bracelet in a leaf design with pale pink rhinestone accents. Courtesy of Cleora Craw.
$95-125.

CHAPTER 11

Coveted Cameos and Incredible Intaglios

Faux tortoise shell cameo pendant brooch, five-link bracelet and clip earrings demi-parure highlighted with Colorado topaz open back navettes and glistening chatons. Author's collection. $275-350.

Rare and beautiful carved intaglio pink rose demi-parure consisting of side hinge clamper brace-let, pendant brooch and clip earrings. Each rose intaglio has multi-faceted edges that pull every color of the rainbow into the theme of this fabulous ensemble. Fuchsia chatons and amethyst open back navettes with pink hued aurora borealis highlights add to the luminosity of this rare beauty. Courtesy of Debrah Mowat. $850-1150.

Graceful fuchsia cameo demi-parure of two tiered pendant brooch and clip earrings. The elegant ruby velvet ribbon surrounding the brooch mimics the soft dance of the lovely Maidens. Ensembles with velvet ribbon were manufactured for only a brief period of time. Courtesy of Debra Trent. $175-225.

Romantic Juliana hang-tagged iridescent mocha cameo parure with five-link bracelet, clip earrings, two tiered pendant brooch and necklace. Highlights of frosted fuchsia and ice blue flow through each silhouette surrounded by hand applied gold paint accenting each beautiful cameo. Colorado topaz chatons and open back navettes complete this breathtaking ensemble. Author's collection. Photo by Richard A. Stoner. $900-1000.

Beautiful ivory cameo silhouette seems to float against Colorado light topaz marquis and paste set chatons. The multiple rhinestone encrusted swirls and hints of hyacinth rhinestones add to the dimensional look of this tiered brooch and clip earrings demi-parure. Courtesy of Debra Trent. $200-250.

Luscious peridot green rhinestones seem to cast an iridescent hue against the lovely cameo silhouette encased within this delicate brooch. Courtesy of Debra Trent. $95-125.

Breathtaking faux tortoise shell double tiered pendant brooch and five-link bracelet demi-parure encased with dark Colorado chatons accented with black matt rhinestones which seem to enhance the darker swirls of colors running throughout this stunning ensemble. Courtesy of Debrah Mowat. $350-400.

Layers of gilded gold leaves encase the lovely centerpiece in this sparkling iridescent intaglio demi-parure. The pendant brooch has a beautiful silhouette carved from the back in reverse with an intense watermelon finish. Aurora borealis chatons encase both the pendant and matching dangle earrings. Author's collection. $200-250.

Emerald green iridescent cameo pendant brooch with gentle swirls of fuchsia and ice blue rhinestones accented with forest green and olivine chatons. Courtesy of Debra Trent. $75-125.

Elegant chocolate marbled cameo demi-parure with five-link bracelet, pendant brooch and clip earrings with soft butterscotch chatons and smoky topaz open back navettes. Author's collection. Photo by Richard A. Stoner. $275-325.

Exquisite reverse carved intaglio demi-parure with double tiered brooch framed with two rows of aurora borealis chatons and matching earrings. All colors of the rainbow come to the surface when light is refracted off this beautiful suite. Courtesy of Debrah Mowat. $150-200.

Lovely rose pink cameo demi-parure with side hinge clamper bracelet, two tiered pendant brooch and clip earrings. Cream colored satin glass silhouettes have a slight pale pink opaque hue to them which contrast beautifully against the deep antique rose chatons. Courtesy of Debra Trent. $600-675.

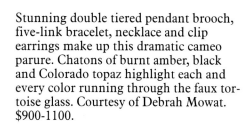

Stunning double tiered pendant brooch, five-link bracelet, necklace and clip earrings make up this dramatic cameo parure. Chatons of burnt amber, black and Colorado topaz highlight each and every color running through the faux tortoise glass. Courtesy of Debrah Mowat. $900-1100.

Wonderful and rare Nefertiti intaglio demi-parure. Tiered
tassel pendant brooch with gold paint applied in reverse
depicting the face of the Egyptian Queen. Matching clip
earrings with unfoiled red navettes and aurora borealis
chatons complete the suite. Courtesy of Debrah Mowat.
$225-275.

Complex two tiered cameo brooch with stunning black silhouette set against
white is framed with multiple levels of black open back navettes and aurora
borealis chatons. Courtesy of Debrah Mowat. $95-115.

Gorgeous sapphire blue cameo clamper bracelet with two complimenting pendant brooches. The creamy pale blue silhouettes make a dramatic statement against the deep cobalt blue glass. Layers of sapphire blue chatons and pale blue rhinestones add the final touch to this beautiful suite. Courtesy of Debra Trent. $500-600.

Intricately carved slag glass topaz cameo demiparure with clamper bracelet, pendant brooch and clip earrings. Each cameo silhouette is surrounded by openwork carved glass in a lacy Victorian theme. Colorado topaz open back navettes are layered throughout with pale citrine and hyacinth chatons. Author's collection. Photo by Richard A. Stoner. $450-500.

Stunning
carved black
glass cameo
demi-parure
of brooch and
clip earrings
with pewter
silhouette.
The surround-
ing elements
include black
faceted marquis
rhinestones
and clear cha-
tons dappled
throughout
elegant loops.
Courtesy of
Debrah Mowat.
$150-200.

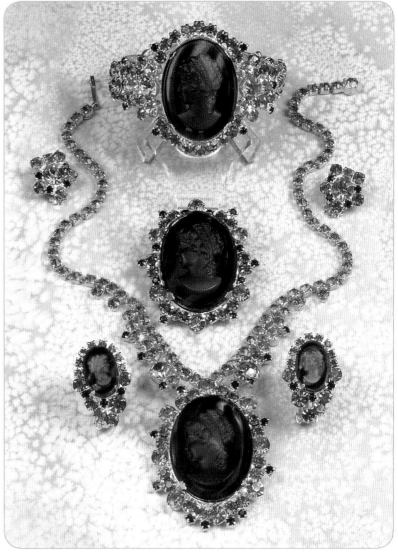

Marble faux tortoise shell cameo grand
parure of necklace, pendant brooch,
hinged clamper bracelet and two styles
of earrings. Deep citrine chatons are interspersed with layers of topaz and black
rhinestones in this remarkable parure fit
for a Queen. Author's collection. Photo
by Richard A. Stoner. $950-1100.

Majestic aqua blue Cameo and dangle earrings demi-parure with layers of glistening chatons in teal blue that enhance the iridescent colors layered throughout the lovely cameo silhouette. Courtesy of Debra Trent. $225-275.

Dramatic Juliana hang-tagged ghost Intaglio clamper bracelet and coordinating brooch demi-parure. Both pieces have a beautiful silhouette carved from the back in reverse with a frosted glass effect beneath the face. Etched gun metal finding is embellished with clear rhinestone navettes and chatons. Author's collection. $275-350.

Rare Nefertiti intaglio pendant brooch with cascading gold tassle and accents of deep amber open back navettes and aurora borealis chatons. The Queen's face is carved in reverse and layered with gold. Author's collection. $150-175.

Graceful cameo tiered brooch and clip earrings demi-parure with amethyst chatons interspersed with matt rose chatons. The cameo silhouette has an iridescent glow to it that pulls the gentle pink surrounding colors into it. Courtesy of Debrah Mowat. $125-175.

Unique intaglio necklace with detailed etching surrounding the pale white silhouette. Cognac rhinestones and gilded gold accents bring attention to the soft
glow eminating from the beautiful face. Courtesy of Debrah Mowat. $175-200.

This delicate ensemble includes a brooch with a bail that is miniature in size and
seems very fitting for a child with complimentary earrings in a watermelon intaglio demi-parure that radiates bright fuchsia, red and peridot with aurora borealis
accents. Author's collection. $75-125.

Beautiful iridescent cameo parure with clamper bracelet, necklace, brooch and rare dangle earrings is surrounded by topaz chantons and open back navettes in this mysteriously gorgeous color combination. Courtesy of Debrah Mowat. $675-775.

CHAPTER 12

Dramatic Dangles

Rare and luscious Siam ruby red parure with clusters of cascading ruby red faceted aurora borealis dangles interspersed throughout the lovely bib necklace, five-link bracelet and clip earrings. Large open back pear shape rhinestones and pointy navettes are mounted between flashes of aurora borealis rhinestones. This set absolutely takes your breath away. Author's collection. Photo by Richard A. Stoner. $1600-1800.

The author performing, while wearing a red Juliana aurora borealis crystal parure. Private collection.
Photo by Jennifer Gregory.

Delightful dangles fall in clusters through-out this colorful demi-parure. Dangles are flocked with various speckles in colors of fuchsia, blue and white with accents of matt turquoise, Capri blue and aurora borealis chatons. Courtesy of Debrah Mowat. $150-225.

Dramatic necklace, five-link brace-let and clip earrings parure loaded with gold swirled and glistening aurora borealis faceted dangles. The necklace has five large clus-ters of dangles suspended from the rhinestone chain. Touches of crystal dangles, open back navettes and aurora borealis chatons make this ensemble a knock out! Courtesy of Linda Munn. $900-1200.

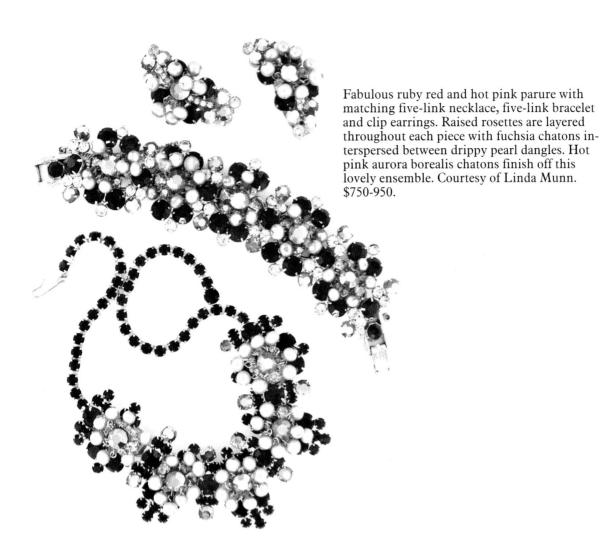

Fabulous ruby red and hot pink parure with matching five-link necklace, five-link bracelet and clip earrings. Raised rosettes are layered throughout each piece with fuchsia chatons interspersed between drippy pearl dangles. Hot pink aurora borealis chatons finish off this lovely ensemble. Courtesy of Linda Munn. $750-950.

Wonderful art glass "seed pod" dangles flow throughout this brooch and clip earrings demi-parure with combinations of Colorado topaz, hyacinth and aurora borealis chatons. Courtesy of Debrah Mowat. $185-225.

Enchanting side hinge clamper style bracelet loaded with clusters of faceted aurora borealis dangles and shining rhinestone navettes and chatons. Courtesy of Cleora Craw. $185-225.

Enticing smoky grey rhinestones are the foundation for this amazing display of aurora borealis faceted dangles layered throughout this fabulous necklace, bracelet and clip earrings parure. Courtesy of Linda Munn. $625-700.

Cascading bib necklace and tiered brooch demi-parure with swirled art glass dangles in Siam red and jet black fall graciously off this rare multi-dimensional masterpiece with raised rosettes and aurora borealis chaton accents. Courtesy of Linda Munn. $750-850.

Lovely demi-parure with tiered brooch and matching clip earrings layered with iridescent crackle glass dangles in ice blue, lavender, pinks and greens with a touch of aurora borealis chatons. Note the creamy white molded givré art glass navettes. Courtesy of Debrah Mowat. $95-125.

Burnt amber open back navettes highlight the stunning amber pear multi-faceted rhinestone at the peak of this lovely brooch. Black dangles drape from the center with black accent chatons all set in japanned metal. Courtesy of Debrah Mowat. $75-100.

Beautiful brooch with flowing black molded art glass flowers accented with a single faceted aurora borealis dangle. Courtesy of Debra Trent. $85-105.

Lovely brooch and earrings demi-parure with gorgeous iridescent peacock art glass dangles layered throughout. Black open back navettes, Colorado topaz chatons and aurora borealis rhinestones add the finishing touch to this beautiful ensemble. Courtesy of Cleora Craw. $150-180.

Iridescent Bermuda blue aurora borealis dangles are layered throughout this exquisite parure of necklace, five-link bracelet, brooch and dangle earrings. Clusters of dangles fall between delicate gold cups with center blue chaton accents and open back blue navettes. The necklace is secured with a gold mesh chain. Courtesy of Debrah Mowat. $625-725.

Elegant faceted aurora borealis crystal necklace, brooch, five-link bracelet and clip earrings parure. Glistening Aurora Borealis faceted dangles cascade throughout this stunning set reflecting every color of the rainbow. Courtesy of Debrah Mowat. $400-500.

Rare and luscious Siam ruby red parure with clusters of cascading ruby red faceted aurora borealis dangles interspersed throughout the lovely bib necklace, five-link bracelet and clip earrings. Large open back pear shape rhinestones and pointy navettes are mounted between flashes of aurora borealis rhinestones. This set absolutely takes your breath away. Author's collection. Photo by Richard A. Stoner. $1600-1800.

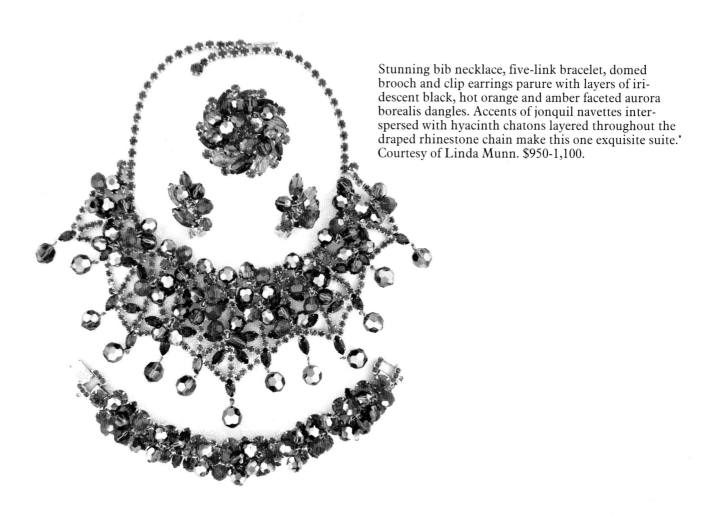

Stunning bib necklace, five-link bracelet, domed brooch and clip earrings parure with layers of iridescent black, hot orange and amber faceted aurora borealis dangles. Accents of jonquil navettes interspersed with hyacinth chatons layered throughout the draped rhinestone chain make this one exquisite suite.' Courtesy of Linda Munn. $950-1,100.

Beautiful five-link bracelet encased with multi-blue art glass seed pod dangles. Open back Capri blue navettes and chatons with a touch of aurora borealis rhinestones call attention to every detail in this playful bracelet. Courtesy of Debrah Mowat. $200-250.

Lustrous molded art glass leaves are accented with matching givré cabochons and cascading drops of pearl and faceted aurora borealis clusters in this elegant demi-parure of brooch, clamper bracelet and clip earrings. Courtesy of Cleora Craw. $275-325.

Lovely pair of iridescent aurora borealis faceted dangle brooches laced with crystal clear chatons. Author's collection. $65-85 each.

Intense pink aurora borealis faceted dangles cascade between gilded gold cups with center pink chaton accents. Open back pink navettes carry the theme through each demi-parure consisting of two unique brooch styles, dangle earrings and clip earrings. Courtesy of Debrah Mowat. $175-225 each set.

Magnificent bib necklace, five-link bracelet and dangle earrings parure with dramatic rhinestone segments layered with clusters of pearls and aurora borealis dangles interspersed with clear chaton encrusted horse-shoe accents. Courtesy of Linda Munn. $675-775.

Dramatic necklace, five-link bracelet, clip earrings and brooch parure layered with cascading jet black faceted dangles with an articulated sweeping leaf motif done in open back jet black chatons. Ice white rhinestones set off the drama in this beautiful ensemble. Photo by Richard A. Stoner. Author's collection. $675-725.

Rich Colorado topaz open back un-foiled pear rhinestones set the scene in this tantalizing brooch and earrings demi-parure layered with cognac aurora borealis dangles, navettes and touches of AB chatons. As viewed throughout this chapter, this particular design was also manufactured in Ruby Red and Bermuda Blue and has been found in Watermelon as well. Courtesy of Debrah Mowat. $250-350.

Iridescent crystal aurora borealis faceted dangles are layered within this beautiful necklace, five-link bracelet, brooch and earrings parure. Cascading grape clusters flow throughout the ensemble with accents of crystal marquis and silvery chatons. Author's collection. Photo by Richard A. Stoner. $475-575.

Highly sought after "Carmen Miranda" seed pod dangle five-link bracelet, tiered brooch and clip earrings demi-parure in rich mustard, burnt tangerine and lime green shades layered with peridot, hyacinth and cognac chatons with a touch of aurora borealis rhinestones. Author's collection. $375-450.

Rare and magnificent parure set with dramatic iridescent heliotrope disks and dangles. The five-link bracelet, cascading necklace and dangle earrings are all accented with large purple givré chatons that set off the luminous fire within this inimitable ensemble. Courtesy of Linda Munn. $850-950.

CHAPTER 13

Elaborate Easter Eggs, Painted Flowers and Magnificent Mother Nature

Magnificent Easter Egg parure with necklace, five-link bracelet, domed brooch and earrings. Elaborate Easter egg cabochons in green, white, blue and gold stippled relief work are the center focus in this wonderfully constructed ensemble. Open back Bermuda and Montana blue navettes are accented with large aurora borealis rhinestones with touches of fuchsia, blue and purple. Courtesy of Linda Munn. $2300-2700.

Author wearing a Juliana Easter Egg parure before a performance. Private collection.
Photo by Jennifer Gregory.

Beautiful Italian marble art glass cabochons grace this lovely demi-parure with rare and unusual cascading pendant brooch and clip earrings. Large faux marble stones are surrounded by Colorado topaz chatons and marquis rhinestones. Floating topaz hued aurora borealis rosettes add to the multi-dimensional construction. Courtesy of Debrah Mowat. $325-375.

Fabulous Easter Egg demi-parure with dramatic dangle earrings, domed brooch, and five-link bracelet. Beautiful fall colors in rich olivine, Colorado topaz and citrine surround the stippled relief work Easter Egg cabochons that display colors of orange, green, peach and gold with iridescent aurora borealis accents. Courtesy of Debrah Mowat. $600-750.

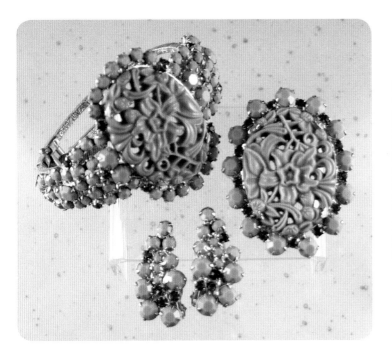

Exquisite faux turquoise demi-parure with side-hinge clamper bracelet, pendant brooch and earrings. The focal point of this beautiful set is the magnificent carved art glass cabochon on the bracelet with cut-out relief work in an oriental theme. Teal blue chatons accent the layers of faux turquoise milk glass rhinestones. Courtesy of Debra Trent. $450-500.

Stupendous and rare Easter Egg parure in iridescent hues of pink, cobalt blue, lavendar and gold with a lavish display of aurora borealis accents. Complete with five-link bracelet, necklace, domed pendant brooch and earrings, this parure takes you into a magical kingdom. Courtesy of Cleora Craw. $1400-1700.

Author performing, wearing a Juliana Easter Egg parure. Private collection. Photo by Jennifer Gregory.

Faux carnelian five-link bracelet with clear open back navettes and rhinestone rosettes encased throughout the links. Author's collection. Photo by Richard A. Stoner. $95-125.

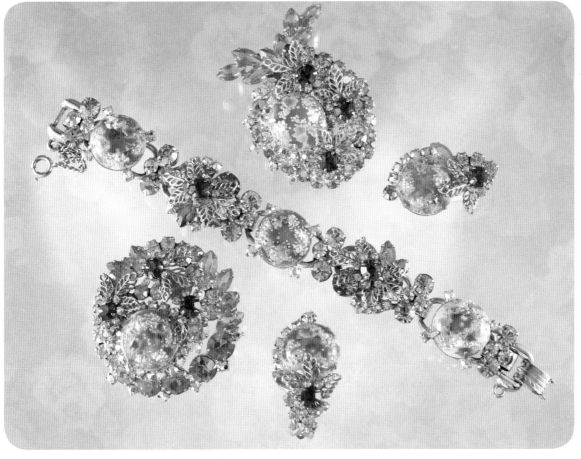

Extraordinary combinations of peridot, hot pink, fuchsia and soft pink grace the beautiful Easter egg cabochons in this tantalizing five-link bracelet and clip earrings demi-parure with two brooches. Accents of filigree leaves are layered throughout that emphasize the bright gold stippling from the Easter egg cabochons. Courtesy of Debra Trent. $625-725.

Drippy faux turquoise art glass stones and lovely rolled gold rope accents are the highlights in this Juliana hang-tagged demi-parure with matching tiered brooch and earrings. Note the faux variegated turquoise stones that truly mimic Mother Nature in all her glory. Courtesy of Debrah Mowat. $175-250.

Amazing faux aventurine gold fluss pear shaped art glass stones are filled with copper powder which is poured directly into the glass resulting in layers of intense gold veining throughout these toffee coloured stones. Highlights of light Colorado topaz and jonquil rhinestones are the finishing touch to this beautiful five-link bracelet, tiered brooch and clip earrings demi-parure. Courtesy of Debrah Mowat. $325-400.

Delicate tiered brooch and clip earrings demi-parure with hand painted flower cabochons in creamy colors of fuchsia, orange, burgundy, jonquil and gold with black stippling. Accents of pink navettes, marquis and aurora borealis rhinestones flow throughout this beautiful labor intensive design. Courtesy of Debra Trent. $275-325.

Incredible Easter egg demi-parure mounted with beautiful aquamarine open back navettes and aurora borealis chatons that pull from the jonquil, burgundy, teal blue and creamy Easter egg cabochons. Complete with five-link bracelet, domed brooch and rare dangle earrings, this suite takes your breath away. Courtesy of Debra Trent. $650-750.

Exquisite faux Italian marble art glass cabachons are layered between golden amber marquis, chatons and aurora borealis rhinestones in this dramatic five-link bracelet, tiered brooch and clip earrings ensemble. Courtesy of Debrah Mowat. $450-525.

Graceful painted flowers dangle earrings with peridot rhinestone accents framing each lovely color filled art glass cabochon. Author's collection. $70-85.

Elegant round Easter egg cabochons in burnt Madeira with white, yellow and green stippling are accented by jonquil and green chatons with a splash of aurora borealis highlights and honey topaz navettes. Large pinwheel style brooch, clip earrings and five-link bracelet complete this stunning ensemble. Courtesy of Cleora Craw. $425-525.

Faux turquoise Art Deco style brooch and clip earrings demi-parure with breathtaking teal blue chaton accents. Courtesy of Debra Trent. $125-155.

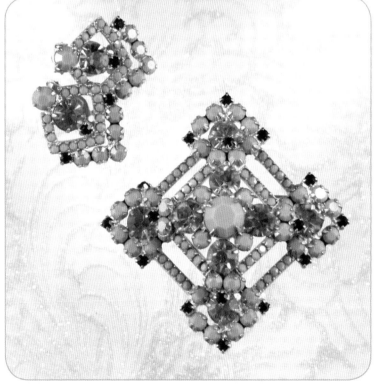

Glistening faux hematite demi-parure with five-link bracelet, pendant brooch and dangle earrings look like the real thing. Highly polished concaved hematite stones are graced by sparkling navettes and rhinestone accents mounted within a japanned metal setting. Courtesy of Cleora Craw. $275-350.

Extravagant faux hematite parure with necklace, five-link bracelet, clip earrings and tiered brooch absolutely takes your breath away. I had a hard time sending this back to its rightful owner after photographing it. It is one you must see in real life. Polished faux hematite stones are surrounded by cognac, peridot, jonquil and emerald green rhinestones with aurora borealis chaton accents. Exquisite. Courtesy of Cleora Craw. $625-725.

Beautiful faux aventurine copper fluss demi-parure with coordinating tiered brooch, five-link bracelet and clip earrings. White matt navettes displayed against iridescent copper coated aurora borealis and Colorado topaz chatons lend the final accents to this elegant suite. Author's collection. Photo by Richard A. Stoner. $250-325.

Elaborate Easter egg cabochons in Tuscan orange with emerald green and canary yellow stippling are accented by deep green chatons and light Colorado topaz open back navettes. Aurora borealis rhinestones add light and luster to this five-link bracelet, large domed brooch and clip earrings demi-parure. Courtesy of Debra Trent. $425-550.

Luminous faux hematite multi-dimensional brooch with contrasting layers of dark and light Colorado topaz navettes and chatons gracing the center raised rosette. Courtesy of Debrah Mowat. $75-95.

Exquisite hand painted flower cabochons in coral, green, fuchsia and burgundy with black stippling set the tone for this incredible five-link bracelet and pendant brooch demi-parure. Open back pink navettes and chatons with a hint of aurora borealis rhinestones tie this bundle up into one extraordinary ensemble. Courtesy of Debrah Mowat. $675-775.

Bold and dramatic faux hematite parure with necklace, domed brooch, five-link bracelet and clip earrings is graced with a mingling of open back smoky navettes, marquis and aurora borealis rhinestones. Note the detailed multidimensional construction in this elaborate ensemble. Courtesy of Debra Trent. $725-850.

Another gorgeous example of stippled Easter egg cabochons displayed in this beautiful tiered brooch and clip earring demi-parure with mesmerizing aurora borealis chatons and hyacinth accents. Courtesy of Debrah Mowat. $200-300.

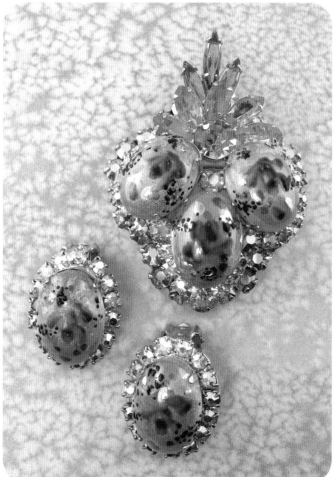

Highly sought after and coveted Easter egg parure with large collar, domed brooch and clip earrings. This massive suite incorporates large open back emerald green pear shape rhinestones accented with Colorado topaz, peridot, emerald green and hyacinth chatons. The extraordinary Easter egg cabochons speak for themselves. Author's collection. Photo by Richard A. Stoner. $1550-2000.

Lovely hand painted flower cabochons nestled between a lower layer of iridescent pink aurora borealis chatons followed by an upper layer of iridescent green aurora borealis chatons in the pendant brooch. Amethyst and pink open back marquis and navettes compliment the coordinating earrings in this demure demi-parure. Courtesy of Cleora Craw. $285-350.

Lavish faux moonstone cabochons supported by rolled gold rope accents and layers of clear marquis rhinestones are the crowning elements in this lovely dangle brooch and clip earrings demi-parure. Courtesy of Cleora Craw. $225-250.

Mesmerizing hand painted flowers demi-parure with brooch and rare dangle earrings blended with aurora borealis rhinestones and Colorado topaz marquis, navettes and chatons. Courtesy of Debrah Mowat. $350-425.

Gorgeous Easter Egg domed brooch and clip earrings demi-parure offering yet another variation of rhinestones in hyacinth, emerald green and smokey citrine with a touch of aurora borealis chatons. Decadant Easter eggs are layered with Tuscan orange, emerald green, gold and canary yellow stippling. Courtesy of Cleora Craw. $250-300.

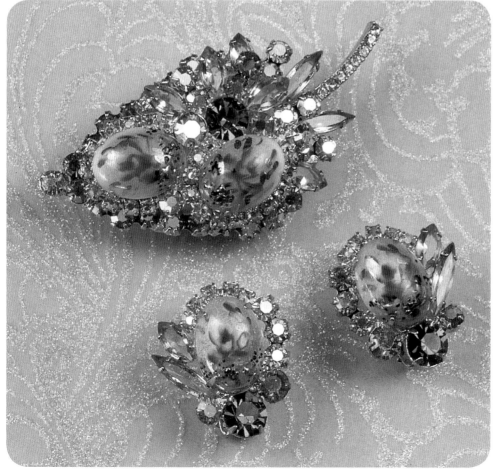

Magical hand painted flowers demi-parure of pendant brooch and clip earrings with peridot marquis and open back navettes, iridescent aurora borealis chatons and a hint of pink rhinestones. Author's collection. Photo by Richard A. Stoner. $275-325.

Delicate gold filigree leaves and aurora borealis chatons capture the colors of the gold graining throughout the lovely faux Italian marble art glass stones in this beautiful brooch and clip earrings demi-parure. Courtesy of Debrah Mowat. $175-225.

Rapturous Siam red marquis rhinestones seem to dance off the glistening faux hematite pear shaped stones. Accents of a deeper red chaton are laced with iridescent aurora borealis beauties in one magnificent five-link bracelet, domed brooch and clip earrings demi-parure. Courtesy of Debra Trent. $400-500.

Superb faux turquoise demi-parure with yet another style of clip earrings and coordinating side-hinge clamper bracelet. Large carved art glass cabochon in an oriental theme is once again the central focus in this elaborate work of art. Layers of faux turquoise milk glass rhinestones are accented with teal blue chatons. Courtesy of Cleora Craw. $300-350.

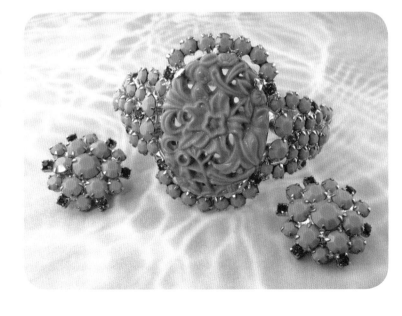

Hand painted flowers in yet another color combination. Striking aurora borealis chatons in multiple layers are accented with citrine marquis and amber navettes adding depth to the glorious painted flower cabochons in this pendant brooch and clip earrings demi-parure. Courtesy of Debra Trent. $295-$350.

Beautiful faux moonstoon clamper bracelet with fire-engine red aurora borealis chatons layered throughout the top and sides. Author's collection. $95-125

Unique purple Easter egg brooch and clip earrings demi-parure with large Montana blue rhinestones and contrasting emerald green marquis with aurora borealis accents set the stage in this wonderful set. Courtesy of Debra Trent. $225-250.

CHAPTER 14
Fabulous Figurals

Adorable pair of turtle brooches featuring large watermelon tourmaline backs. Ms. Turtle is dressed in bright pink chatons with amethyst accents while her mate is layered with Montana blue chatons in a japanned setting, both with aurora borealis accents. Notice the floating, wire-over eyes. Author's collection. $140-175 each.

Stunning margarita encased butterfly brooch with green and hyacinth navettes surrounded by Bermuda blue and Colorado topaz chatons. Courtesy of Debrah Mowat. $225-300.

Fantastic collection of diverse turtle brooches with watermelon tourmaline backs. Colors range from Colorado topaz, Bermuda blue, aquamarine and hyacinth to Siam red. Intense Emerald green lizard brooch is highlighted with iridescent green aurora borealis chatons. Courtesy of Debrah Mowat. $140-350 each.

Figural donkey proudly displays three hand painted sugar bead dangles surrounded by Colorado topaz chatons with rich amber navette ears. Courtesy of Debrah Mowat. $95-110.

Beautiful pair of margarita double tiered owl brooches with navettes, marquis and chatons ranging in color from Bermuda blue to Colorado topaz. A must have for every collection. Courtesy of Debrah Mowat. $150 each.

Close up of Mr. Lizard displaying his colors to the hilt! Note the wire over eyes set with rich aurora borealis chatons and the distinctive feet with one large center chaton surrounded by three complimentary rhinestones. Courtesy of Debrah Mowat. $300-350

Whimsical road runner brooch in Montana and Bermuda blue rhinestones with glistening aurora borealis accents looks like he's headed for trouble! Courtesy of Cleora Craw. $75-100.

Beautiful example of japanned owl brooches with mesmerizing margarita eyes and layers of open back navettes on each crown. Colors range from jonquil, fuchsia and peridot to Siam ruby all highlighted with aurora borealis chatons. Courtesy of Debra Trent. $150-200 each.

Parrot demi-parure with brooch and matching earrings. Large pear topaz rhinestone belly with wonderful display of pointy navettes as feathers in topaz and green. A single raised rosette accents each piece with multiple layers of aurora borealis chatons. Courtesy of Debrah Mowat. $225.

Close up of two turtle brooches displaying detail of wire-over eyes. Author's collection. $140-175 each.

Amazing peacock brooch with huge tourmaline watermelon center surrounded by aurora borealis chatons. Elaborate multi dimensional feather spray of Capri blue navettes and green marquis mimic the colors throughout the head and neck. Courtesy of Debra Trent. $175-225.

Fantastic butterfly brooch with large tourmaline watermelon stones gracing each wing. Colorado topaz chatons, pale cognac marquis and hyacinth navettes contrast beautifully against the emerald green and aurora borealis rhinestones. Courtesy of Debrah Mowat. $225-250.

Turtle Debutant Ball! Lovely display of four turtle brooches with a contrasting mix of rhinestones in every color of the rainbow. Courtesy of Debrah Mowat. $145-165 each.

Glorious mandolin figural instrument brooch with a deep Siam red rhinestone center and top, surrounded by flashing aurora borealis chatons. Courtesy of Cleora Craw. $90-105.

Lustrous peacock brooch in yet another unique color combination. Huge tourmaline watermelon stone is surrounded by aurora borealis chatons with layers of teal and Bermuda blue navettes dancing from the raised rosette center throughout the rest of his feathered body. Photo by Debrah Mowat. Courtesy of Lynn Compton. $175-225.

Fantastic Siam red rivoli japanned owl brooch with layers of rhinestones in pinks and reds with a touch of hyacinth. Deep ruby red chatons surround each rivoli eye. Courtesy of Debra Trent. $185.

Back view of japanned owl brooch displaying metal work, open navettes and built-in pin assembly. Note the fluted edge cup mountings. Courtesy of Debra Trent. $185.

Hot pink rhinestone turtle brooch with tourmaline watermelon belly surrounded by large pink chatons and smaller pink chatons in the bottom layer. Amethyst face displays glistening aurora borealis wire-over eyes. Author's collection. $140.

Inimitable watermelon margarita owl
brooch and earrings demi-parure.
Contrasting shades of green rhinestones
and aurora borealis chatons surround
the intense margarita focal stones in this
gorgeous set. Courtesy of Debra Trent.
$275.

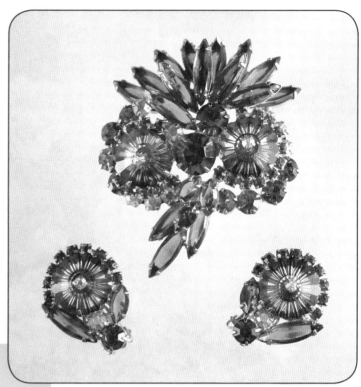

Spectacular rooster figural brooch with such a
glorious display of feathers in Capri blue navettes
with smaller blue marquis accents. Layer upon
layer of blue and green chatons are mixed with a
gentle spray of aurora borealis rhinestones that
seem to dance around the large tourmaline watermelon belly. Courtesy of Debrah Mowat. $185-200.

Playful kitty cat brooch with large Siam red
head, eyes, ears, nose and whiskers. Large
watermelon tourmaline belly is accented with
Siam red rhinestones while subtle layers of
aurora borealis chatons grace her lovely head.
Courtesy of Debrah Mowat. $200.

Wonderful rare japanned turtle brooch with large Bermuda blue chatons layered with ice blue aurora borealis chatons. Note the intricate scalloped rhinestone edge that is a prominent element in the turtle figural brooches. Author's collection. $165.

Stunning watermelon margarita butterfly brooch and clip earrings demi-parure with layers of teal green open back navettes and marquis rhinestones highlighted with citrine, hyacinth and teal chatons. Courtesy of Debrah Mowat. $200-250.

Two delightful bug brooches with lovely gold wings, raised rosette accents and layers of contrasting open and closed back rhinestones. Courtesy of Debrah Mowat. $70-90 each.

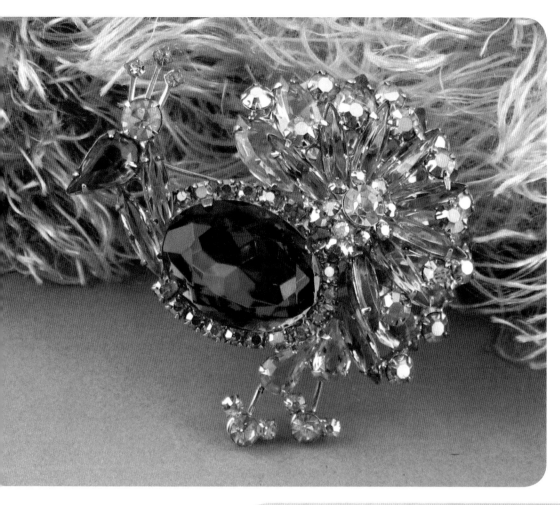

Flamboyant peacock brooch with heliotrope watermelon belly, raised rosette accent and lovely feather display in pale green and aquamarine open back navettes. The colors continue throughout the piece with layers of glistening aurora borealis chatons. Author's collection. $175-250.

Close up of watermelon rivoli owl brooch with pink, green, topaz, hyacinth and aurora borealis rhinestones. Courtesy of Debrah Mowat. $135-165.

Wonderful watermelon back turtle brooch with Capri blue and Montana blue chatons and aurora borealis wire-over eyes. Courtesy of Debrah Mowat. $145.

Amazing bright fuchsia rivoli owl brooch and clip earrings demi-parure. Multiple shades of pink and fuchsia navettes, marquis and chatons bring out every radiating hue within the glorious rivoli rhinestones. Courtesy of Debra Trent. $185-250.

Meeting of two like minds! Extravagantly embellished japanned lizard brooches in contrasting colors. Forefront lizard is dressed in hyacinth chatons with aurora borealis spine. Foreground lizard displays bright emerald green chatons with aurora borealis spine. Note the wire-over eyes and rhinestone scalloped edging in these rare and unique beauties. Courtesy of Debrah Mowat. $275-300 each.

Back view of japanned lizard brooches displaying metal work, wire-over, open navettes, rivet/eyelets and built-in pin assembly. Courtesy of Debrah Mowat. $275-325 each.

Intense tourmaline water-melon turtle brooch and clip earrings demi-parure with layers of Montana blue, cobalt blue and teal blue rhinestones. Courtesy of Debrah Mowat. $175-275.

Magical grouping of mandolin, cello and violin figural instrument brooches. Red mandolin with large Siam ruby center stone and highlights of aurora borealis chatons, large cello in flashing layers of neon blue aurora borealis chatons and detailed gold gilt strings followed by an exquisite example of smoke grey rhinestones in a very elegant violin brooch. Courtesy of Cleora Craw. $120-140.

Beautiful deep Colorado topaz owl brooch and earrings demi-parure with aurora borealis rhinestone rosettes, large open back navettes and burnt amber highlights. Courtesy of Debrah Mowat. $175-225.

Exquisite and rare dragonfly tiered figural brooch with enormous wing span layered in teal blue and Bermuda blue navettes and chatons with lovely Montana blue keystones as the front wing focal point. Courtesy of Debrah Mowat. $225-275.

Eye popping combinations of Capri blue molded art glass marquis and bright salmon layered givré stones make this one regal butterfly brooch. Deep ruby red chaton accents grace the center body and wings. Courtesy of Cleora Craw. $100-125.

Lovely amethyst owl brooch and earrings demi-parure with
magnificent watermelon margaritas. This set truly looks like
it is ready to fly with its multitude of deep amethyst open back
navettes and marquis rhinestones dappled with layers of burgundy and purple chatons and aurora borealis accents. Courtesy
of Debra Trent. $195-250.

Adoption papers signed, sealed and delivered! Side view of two japanned lizard brooches
with lovely watermelon backed turtle brooch in a blend of electric blue rhinestones. Courtesy of Debrah Mowat. $145-300.

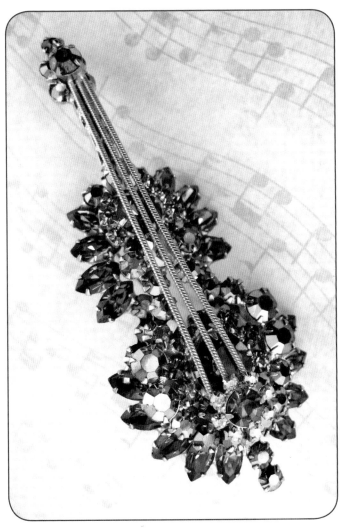

Dramatic cello multi-dimensional brooch with layers of electric blue aurora borealis chatons and Bermuda blue marquis rhinestones set to perfection. The gold gilt metal strings gently flow from a center raised rosette to the detailed rhinestone top. Author's collection. $100-135.

Curious Mr. Crab figural brooch with tourmaline watermelon center, lovely ice-blue open marquis claws with Bermuda blue accents and watery aurora borealis chatons. Rare. Courtesy of Debrah Mowat. $175–250.

How many color combinations did these gorgeous peacocks come in? Two contrasting examples with large watermelon tourmaline centers, dazzling layers of aurora borealis chatons and two tiered wing fans ranging in flashing colors from hot pink layered beneath peridot green to Montana blue layered beneath Capri blue with raised rosette accents. Courtesy of Debrah Mowat. $175-225. each.

Amazing japanned night owl brooch with intense tabac rivoli eyes. Large feather display in contrasting layers of cognac and citrine open back navettes and a final touch of deep ruby chatons. Courtesy of Debra Trent. $165.

Back view of japanned owl brooch demonstrating use of open back navettes and built-in pin assembly with fluted cup mountings. Courtesy of Debra Trent. $165.

Aerial view of three butterfly brooches in contrasting colors, dragonfly brooch and two bug brooches. Note the formidable use of intense and vivid rhinestones throughout each amazing piece. Courtesy of Debrah Mowat. $85-225.

Close up of hyacinth japanned lizard brooch demonstrating fluted aurora borealis rhinestone edging. Courtesy of Debrah Mowat. $275.

Back view of tourmaline watermelon turtle brooch displaying tail and back construction. Courtesy of Debrah Mowat. $140.

Amazing rooster figural brooch employing a bold display of feathers in deep Colorado topaz and chartreuse navettes with smaller cognac and hyacinth marquis accents. Layers of aurora borealis rhinestones accentuate the beautiful watermelon tourmaline belly. Courtesy of Debra Trent. $185-200.

Magnificent Montana blue chatons contrasted with large teal blue rhinestones bring out every color in this little guy's tourmaline watermelon back. Courtesy of Debrah Mowat. $135-155.

Beautiful soaring bird brooch with Siam red belly surrounded by aurora borealis chatons with a lovely wing span in open back pink navettes. Note the large fuschia aurora borealis head and delicate Siam ruby beak. Courtesy of Debra Trent. $95-125.

Highly desirable watermelon rivoli butterfly brooch with layers of tourmaline green open back navettes and marquis with a touch of champagne and hyacinth rhinestone accents. Note the intense heliotrope center of the rivoli rhinestones. Courtesy of Debrah Mowat. $175-250.

Back view of watermelon rivoli butterfly brooch displaying open back navettes and built in pin assembly. Courtesy of Debrah Mowat. $175-250.

Birds of a feather collection with two parrot demi-parures, one owl demi-parure and the Master Peacock showcasing a mesmerizing display of rhinestone feathers. Courtesy of Debrah Mowat. $175-250.

Lovely tabac watermelon turtle brooch with layers of cognac and Colorado topaz chatons and aurora borealis accents. Courtesy of Debrah Mowat. $125-150.

Beguiling watermelon margarita owl brooch and earring demi-parure with beautiful deep sapphire open back navettes at the head and beak. Accents of aurora borealis rhinestones glisten against the contrasting Capri blue chatons and pale blue marquis. Courtesy of Cleora Craw. $225-275.

Colorful crow perched on a gold gilt metal branch with gold filigree wing and every imaginable color of rhinestones encased throughout the lovely body. Note the rhinestone encrusted ball at the foot of the branch adding yet another element of dimension. Courtesy of Debrah Mowat. $85-105.

Magical collection of figural string instrument brooches in contrasting colors of Siam ruby red, smoky gray and heliotrope rhinestones with bold center stone accents. Courtesy of Cleora Craw. $125-150 each.

Rare and remarkable lobster brooch showing off a flashy watermelon back with hints of heliotrope that highlight a glorious display of ice-blue chatons, Capri blue rhinestones and navettes throughout the body. Courtesy of Debrah Mowat. $225-275.

145

CHAPTER 15

Mesmerizing Margaritas, Rapturous Rivoli and Wild Watermelon

This one has it all: a stupendous parure with bib necklace, domed brooch, and clip earrings combining oval watermelon, rivoli and margarita rhinestones interspersed with accents of green marquis, burnt orange and hyacinth chatons. Courtesy of Linda Munn. $2000-2400.

Beautiful tiered brooch and earrings demi-parure in blue watermelon margaritas with highlights of Bermuda blue, Montana blue and ice blue navettes and chatons, all accented with layers of aurora borealis rhinestones. Courtesy of Debra Trent. $250-300.

Large tourmaline watermelon stones are surrounded by amethyst and fuchsia navettes and chatons in this lovely brooch. Courtesy of Debrah Mowat. $110-130.

Incredible margaritas encompassing all the colors of a glorious sunset are the highlight in this radiantly rare domed brooch and bib necklace demi-parure with scalloped edging and layers of navettes and chatons in light Colorado topaz, fuchsia, hot pink and hyacinth. Courtesy of Debra Trent. $950-1200.

Tantalizing watermelon demi-parure with five-link bracelet, multi-dimensional brooch and clip earrings is layered with rhinestone rosettes in gorgeous autumn colors of smoky topaz, forest green and hyacinth with aurora borealis accents. Courtesy of Cleora Craw. $675-850.

Mesmerizing rivoli tiered brooch and clip earrings demi-parure with raised rosette accents are highlighted by aurora borealis rhinestones and and layers of amethyst and Siam red chatons and navettes. Courtesy of Debrah Mowat. $225-250.

Two elaborate rivoli brooch and earrings demi-parures in contrasting designs. Each ensemble is layered with emerald green watermelon rivoli and accents of hunter's green, forest green and mint green chatons, navettes and marquis rhinestones with aurora borealis accents. Courtesy of Debrah Mowat. $200-250 each.

Rare and highly sought after japanned demi-parure in an Art Deco theme with two brooches, two pair of clip earrings, lovely dangle earrings and clamper bracelet. These dramatic pieces are encased with tourmaline watermelon rivoli surrounded by hyacinth, forest green, Capri blue, Colorado topaz and fuchsia rhinestones. Courtesy of Debrah Mowat. $1300-1500.

Japanned Art Deco dangle earrings on original Juliana card.
Courtesy of Debrah Mowat. $150-200.

Beautiful example of three dimensional layering in this lovely flower brooch and
dangle earrings demi-parure. Ruby red Siam brooch is layered with floating wire-
over accents, multiple rhinestone rows and a huge Siam red rivoli tucked in the
center with added touches of fuchsia, berry red and deep burgundy rhinestones.
Courtesy of Debrah Mowat. $175-250.

Deliriously captivating five-link bracelet, tiered brooch, collar necklace and clip earrings parure layered with flashing cobalt blue rivoli rhinestones surrounded by Capri blue navettes, Bermuda blue marquis, teal blue chatons and flickering aurora borealis rhinestones. Courtesy of Linda Munn. $2300-2700.

154

Smoky gray margarita clip earrings with open back ice blue navettes, marquis and aurora borealis accents. Courtesy of Debra Trent. $60-75.

Elegant Siam ruby watermelon rivoli brooch and earrings demi-parure in contrasting layers of deep burgundy, pale amethyst and aurora borealis rhinestones with raised rosette accents. Courtesy of Debra Trent. $225-275.

Intense green margarita necklace, owl brooch and clip earrings demi-parure with luminous colors of fuchsia, lemon, peridot and jonquil highlights dancing off the facets of each margarita and aurora borealis rhinestone. Layers of emerald green chatons combined with marquis and open back navettes are the final accents in this gorgeous suite. Courtesy of Cleora Craw. $750-850.

Multi-tiered brooch and clip earring demi-parure with intense Capri blue watermelon stones surrounded by Montana blue and Bermuda blue rhinestones with layers of aurora borealis and rosette accents. Courtesy of Debrah Mowat. $225-275.

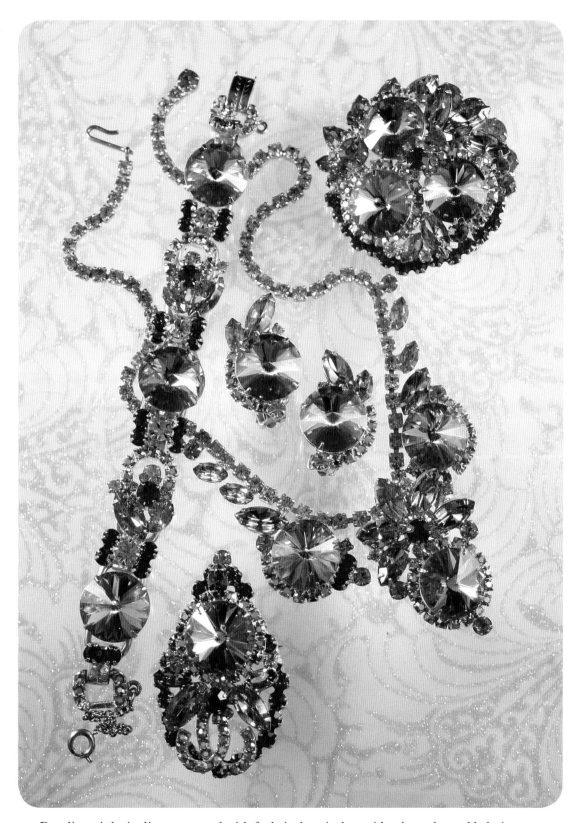

Dazzling pink rivoli are accented with fuchsia, hyacinth, peridot, lavender and balerina pink rhinestones with bright fuchsia aurora borealis accents in this lovely Grand parure of necklace, five-link bracelet, two diverse brooches and clip earrings. If Cinderella was wearing jewelry the night she lost her glass slipper, this was the set. Courtesy of Debra Trent. $1300-1500.

Magnificent multi-tiered brooch with huge green watermelon margarita stones coupled with hints of aurora borealis chatons and layers of rhinestones in olivine and emerald green. Courtesy of Debra Trent. $150-175.

Incredible brooch and earrings demi-parure filled with intense fuchsia and pale lavender rhinestones surrounding each and every iridescent amethyst, fuchsia rivoli and tourmaline watermelon stone displayed within this flashy suite. Courtesy of Debrah Mowat. $175-225.

Delicate heliotrope margarita is encased in a silver filigree cage with accents of Montana blue navettes and sapphire blue and fuschia chatons in this graceful brooch. Author's collection. Photo by Richard A. Stoner. $65-85.

Sweeping layers of green tourmaline margaritas are laced with touches of rich cognac marquis, hyacinth and gold chatons and icy aurora borealis rhinestones in this beautiful five-link bracelet and floral brooch ensemble with two pair of complimenting earrings. Courtesy of Debrah Mowat. $550-650.

Japanned brooch with jonquil, cognac, hyacinth, copper and fuchsia chatons set in multiple layers around five large watermelon rivoli rhinestones. Courtesy of Debrah Mowat. $125-155.

Glistening tiered brooch and earrings demi-parure with peridot green marquis, chatons and margarita rhinestones. Author's collection. Photo by Richard A. Stoner. $125-145.

159

Dramatic watermelon stones are the dreamy highlights in this glorious five-link bracelet, necklace, tiered brooch and clip earrings parure. Rich autumn colors of cognac, topaz, forest green, hyacinth and iridescent aurora borealis rhinestones complete the stage of this lovely ensemble fit for a Queen. Courtesy of Debrah Mowat. $1400–1700.

Stunning combination of smoky blue rivoli with chatons, navettes and marquis rhinestones with aurora borealis accents create yet another masterpiece in this elegant brooch and earrings demi-parure. Courtesy of Debra Trent. $125-155.

Spellbinding presentation of bright fuchsia rivoli stones flocked with amethyst aurora borealis chatons and layers of pink, fuchsia, peridot, hyacinth and lavender rhinestones in this brooch and earrings demi-parure. Courtesy of Debrah Mowat. $200-250.

One beautiful watermelon rhinestone encased under layers of aurora borealis chatons with Montana and Capri blue rhinestones in this incomparable brooch. Courtesy of Debra Trent. $95-125.

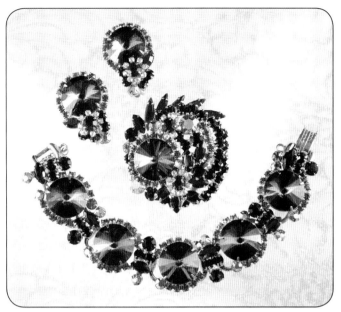

Red volcano rivolvi flash like burning embers throughout this amazing five-link bracelet, tiered brooch and clip earrings parure with floating rosette accents, aurora borealis highlights and layers of cognac, Siam ruby red and deep burgundy rhinestones. Courtesy of Debra Trent. $475-575.

Layers of pink and fuchsia rhinestones surround deep fuchsia margaritas all set in a romantic design in this captivating earrings and brooch demi-parure. Note the lovely cascading navettes flowing from the brooch. Courtesy of Debrah Mowat. $225-275.

This highly sought after watermelon parure encompasses every color of the rainbow. Extremely large watermelon tourmaline open back rhinestones are graced by Bermuda blue, Siam red, peridot and ice blue rhinestones. Note how the aurora borealis chatons are gently caged around each watermelon stone. Courtesy of Linda Munn. $2700-3500.

Luminous polychromatic rivoli stones in oval and round sizes are orchestrated throughout this fantastically feminine brooch, earrings and side-hinge clamper bracelet demi-parure. Aurora borealis chatons blended with hot pink and fuchsia rhinestones delicately add to the sparkle of this lovely ensemble. Author's collection. $450-550.

Two knock-out flower brooch and earrings demi-parures in contrasting colors. One set is covered with margaritas and rhinestones in fall colors while the other suite takes you into the deep waters of the Mediterranean Sea. Courtesy of Debrah Mowat. $275-325 each.

Dramatic volcano red rivoli are surrounded by multiple layers of Siam red, hyacinth, fuchsia and hot pink rhinestones in this sultry tiered brooch and clip earrings demi-parure. Courtesy of Cleora Craw. $225-275.

Floating rhinestone rosettes are interspersed between emerald green watermelon rivoli stones while olivine and emerald green chatons and marquis capture the highlights from the aurora borealis accents in this domed brooch and clip earrings set. Courtesy of Debrah Mowat. $225-250.

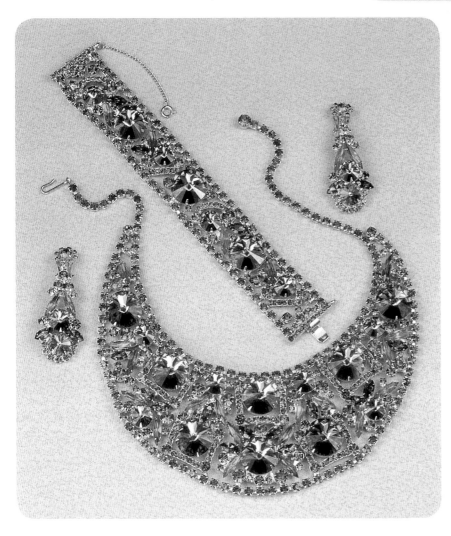

Luscious watermelon rivoli laden bib necklace, flat back bracelet and dangle earrings parure. Note the play of design as each watermelon rivoli is framed with paste set chatons in Colorado topaz. Smaller watermelon rivoli accented with hyacinth, peridot and touches of Madeira rhinestones make this one intoxicating ensemble. Photo by Richard A. Stoner. Author's collection. $1800-2200.

Hot fuchsia rivoli tiered brooch and earrings demi-parure with sparkling pink and burgundy chatons layered throughout. Courtesy of Debra Trent. $250-275.

Tantalizing five-link bracelet, tiered brooch and clip earrings demi-parure are set in a dazzling show with multiple green watermelon margarita stones, raised rosettes with touches of cognac, hyacinth and smoky quartz chatons. Courtesy of Debrah Mowat. $425-525.

Highly sought after watermelon demi-parure with rare dangle earrings, five-link bracelet and domed brooch. Finian's rainbow in living color with large watermelon tourmaline open back rhinestones highlighted with Siam red, peridot, Bermuda blue and arctic blue rhinestones. Courtesy of Debrah Mowat. $900- 1200.

Luscious tourmaline watermelon Juliana hang-tagged necklace, brooch and earrings parure absolutely takes your breath away. The contrast of deep Siam ruby red marquis and chatons against all the sparkling aurora borealis rhinestones sets your heart on fire. Courtesy of Debra Trent. $950-1250.

Fuchsia brooch and earrings demi-parure with hot pink navettes, marquis and chatons are accented by fuchsia tipped aurora borealis rhinestones in this oh-so-feminine set. Courtesy of Debra Trent. $175-225.

Rare and unique triangle watermelon stones are the highlight in this striking dimensional brooch and earrings demi-parure. Note how the hot pink, heliotrope, cognac and jonquil rhinestones pull your eye directly to the center of each watermelon rhinestone in this incomparable design. Courtesy of Debrah Mowat. $275-350.

Fantastic display of Fall colors are incorporated throughout this amazing demi-parure with five-link bracelet, tiered brooch and clip earrings. Hyacinth, Colorado topaz, citrine and Madeira rhinestones seem to dance around the glorious watermelon stones. Another fine example of how the artistic eye of DeLizza and Elster can bring the beating of your heart to a dead stop. Courtesy of Debra Trent. $625-725.

Bold and delicious Bermuda blue rivoli set the stage in this massive tiered brooch and clip earrings demi-parure with floating raised rosettes, teal blue and cobalt blue rhinestones and just the right touch of aurora borealis chatons. Courtesy of Cleora Craw. $250-300.

Intricate multi-dimensional brooch with volcano rivoli, raised rosettes and layers of Siam ruby navettes and marquis combined with cognac and burgundy chatons with a splash of aurora borealis rhinestones. Courtesy of Debrah Mowat. $115-145.

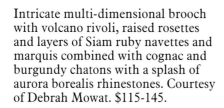

166

Highly sought after and extremely rare tourmaline watermelon collar, five-link bracelet, tiered brooch and clip earrings Grand parure. Layer upon layer of heliotrope navettes, chatons and marquis rhinestones flash like lightening throughout this over the top ensemble. Notice the iridescent aurora borealis swags with articulated dangles flowing off the elaborate collar. Courtesy of Linda Munn. $3000-3500.

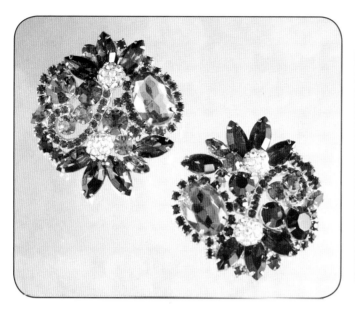

Lovely pair of watermelon brooches carrying the same theme throughout in contrasting colors of Siam red and Capri blue. Note how many rhinestone variations and accents are used throughout each beauty. Courtesy of Debra Trent. $145-165 each.

Vivid volcano red rivoli dangle earrings are multitiered and dressed with Siam red navettes, marquis and chatons with iridescent red aurora borealis accents. Courtesy of Debrah Mowat. $95-125.

Glorious flower brooch and earrings demi-parure grouping with layers of contrasting rhinestones in watermelon, margarita and rivoli with dangles and pinwheel designs and more! Note the excellent examples of floating wire-over accents gracing each flower stem. Courtesy of Debrah Mowat. $175-350 each.

Elaborate multi tiered brooch with watermelon margaritas, raised rosettes and surrounding rhinestones in Colorado topaz, cognac with iridescent aurora borelis chatons. Courtesy of Debra Trent. $175-200.

Deep Bermuda blue watermelon rhinestones are set so beautifully in this multi-dimensional brooch and earrings demi-parure. Aurora borealis, teal blue and Bermuda blue chatons seem to flow through the articulated gold chain accents. Courtesy of Cleora Craw. $175-225.

Bright heliotrope watermelon stones are the eye-catching element in this striking necklace and earrings demi-parure. Layers of Capri blue, teal blue and Montana blue rhinestones perfectly unleash the vitriel luminousity within the grand watermelon stones in this stunning suite. Aurora borealis chatons and raised rosettes add the final touch. Courtesy of Debra Trent. $675-775.

Unbelievable masterpiece with huge bib collar, domed brooch, clamper bracelet and clip earrings. Large and showy display of tourmaline watermelon, rivoli and margarita rhinestones are combined with heliotrope, Siam red, purple, emerald green, fuchsia and deep burgundy chatons and navettes. The layered structure of this fabulously decadent parure absolutely transports you to another dimension of the universe. Courtesy of Linda Munn. $2700-3500.

Radiant rivoli are mounted throughout this fiery Bermuda blue tiered brooch with raised rosette accents interspersed with layers of ice blue, aurora borealis and Montana blue rhinestones. Courtesy of Debra Trent. $145-185.

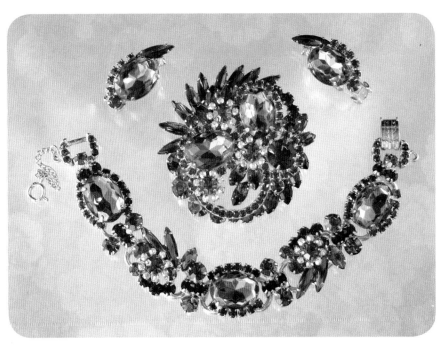

Tantalizing watermelon beauties are displayed within this incredible five-link bracelet, tiered brooch and clip earrings demi-parure. A multitude of rhinestones in contrasting colors of fuchsia, burgundy, purple and amethyst set off the fire in this splendid ensemble. Courtesy of Debra Trent. $650-750.

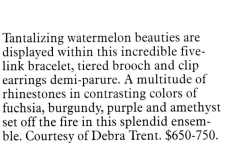

Striking watermelon margarita pendant brooch and earrings demi-parure with multi-dimensional structure showcasing layers of emerald green rhinestones mounted between iridescent peridot aurora borealis chatons. Author's collection. $175-225.

Stunning close-up example of multi-dimensional brooch mounted with layers of olivine navettes, hyacinth and topaz rhinestones with aurora borealis accents cradling each luscious watermelon stone. Courtesy of Debrah Mowat. $155-200.

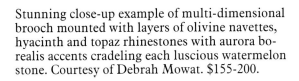

Regal and dramatic collar necklace displaying nineteen peacock watermelon stones with cascading Bermuda blue marquis drops and teal blue accents with accompanying clip earrings. The elaborate watermelon brooch compliments this demi-parure beautifully. Courtesy of Linda Munn. $2700-3100.

Beguiling fuchsia rivoli stones are accented with layers of rose pink and fuchsia rhinestones in this wonderful brooch. Courtesy of Debra Trent. $155-185.

Remarkably glorious heliotrope margarita stones seem to blaze with fire in this tiered brooch, five-link bracelet and clip earrings demi-parure. Note the dramatic use of rhinestones in multiple colors and layers in this stunning suite. Courtesy of Debrah Mowat. $575-675.

Highly desirable and rare pair of japanned brooches in an Art Deco theme with contrasting rhinestones in heliotrope, fuchsia, purple, Bermuda blue, jonquil, teal blue and emerald green. Courtesy of Debrah Mowat. $225-250 each.

173

Flashing emerald green watermelon margarita stones are mounted in a complex design in this knock-out five-link bracelet, tiered brooch, necklace and clip earrings parure. Iridescent green aurora borealis chatons are combined with emerald green navettes and marquis rhinestones throughout this ensemble. Courtesy of Linda Munn. $975-1375.

Dramatically embellished demi-parure with side hinge clamper bracelet, domed brooch and two sets of clip earrings is layered with volcano red rivoli, heliotrope margarita and tourmaline watermelon stones. Accents of purple, Siam ruby, fuchsia and teal green rhinestones reflect off each aurora borealis chaton. All complete with the original Juliana hang-tag. Courtesy of Debra Trent. $850-1150.

Massive tourmaline watermelon collar and clip earring demi-parure. Large emerald green pear shape rhinestones are mounted between swags of aurora borealis chatons with intense hot pink and fuchsia rhinestones pulling from the light within each watermelon stone. This set was also produced in fall colors with green Easter egg cabochons as viewed in chapter thirteen. Courtesy of Linda Munn. $1200-1500.

Beautiful Capri blue tourmaline watermelon stones are surrounded by striking ice blue, Montana blue and olivine rhinestones in a complex layered construction. Shimmering blue aurora borealis rhinestones add to the luminousity of this demi-parure with five-link bracelet, brooch and clip earrings. Courtesy of Debra Trent. $650-700.

Luscious heliotrope margaritas are surrounded by deep amethyst chatons and navettes in this glorious parure with five-link bracelet, pendant brooch, necklace and clip earrings. Fuchsia and aurora borealis accents highlighted with raised rosettes add the final touches to this beauty. Courtesy of Debra Trent. $1000-1200.

Stunning watermelon rivoli demi paurure with glorious domed brooch, flat back bracelet and two pair of earrings including dangles. Bold colors of hyacinth, peridot, smoky quartz and citrine rhinestones are mounted in one fabulous design. Courtesy of Debrah Mowat. $650-850.

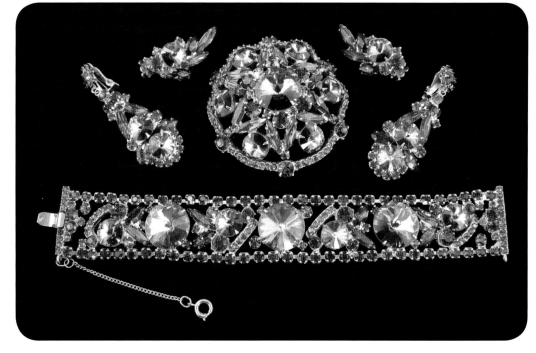

This beautiful set is many times mistaken for watermelon. The large stones are actually a specialty stone that have a vitreil watermelon coating applied to them. Iridescent watermelon hues are prevalent throughout this five-link necklace, five-link bracelet and large multi-dimensional brooch parure. A perfect blend of Montana blue, ice blue and iridescent aurora borealis rhinestones add the finishing touch. Author's collection. Photo by Richard A. Stoner. $525-675.

Exquisite tiered brooch, five-link bracelet and rare dangle earrings demi-parure in Fall colors laced with huge watermelon stones that are set off by a stunning combination of hyacinth, citrine, forest green, Madeira and iridescent aurora borealis rhinestones. The rare and dramatic dangle earring pendants are nearly three inches long. Courtesy of Cleora Craw. $700-800.

Radiantly intense peacock margarita stones are layered throughout this
ultra-feminine parure with cascading necklace, five-link bracelet, tiered
brooch and clip earrings. Highlights of iridescent pink aurora borealis chatons are blended with amethyst marquis and navette rhinestones. Courtesy
of Debrah Mowat. $975-1175.

Iridescent polychromatic rivoli stones in oval and round shapes are the crowning jewels in this
beautiful necklace and clamper bracelet demi-parure. Deep olivine and jonquil rhinestones
compliment the lovely aurora borealis chatons dancing throughout this superb ensemble. Courtesy of Debrah Mowat. $475-575.

Fabulous peacock watermelon stones are orchestrated in multi-dimensional layers throughout this intoxicating necklace, clamper bracelet, brooch and clip earrings parure. Note the rhinestone encrusted balls and teal blue chanton layered half spirals and horseshoes that give this ensemble a very ethereal look. Courtesy of Debra Trent. $1200-1400.

Pale canary yellow rhinestone chain is decorated with cascades of deep Montana blue open back ovals accented with magenta chatons and navettes with multiple emerald green rivoli drops suspended throughout this amazing large bib necklace. Courtesy of Linda Munn. $725-925.

Two lovely tired brooches each displaying unique flowing designs in contrasting colors of Emerald green, Bermuda blue, teal blue, ice blue and fuchsia with iridescent aurora borealis accents and one lovely deep green rivoli center. Author's collection. $65-95 each

CHAPTER 16
Ravishing Rhinestones

Dreamy multi-dimensional parure with beautiful flowing lines. Bermuda blue, emerald green and ice blue rhinestones are highlighted with iridescent aurora borealis chatons in this lovely five-link bracelet, tiered brooch, cascading necklace and clip earrings ensemble graced with rhinestone rosettes. Courtesy of Debra Trent. $1300-1500.

Chunky five-link bracelet in ice blue rhinestones with large iridescent aurora borealis chatons. Author's collection. $95-135.

Rare peridot keyhole demi-parure with original Juliana hangtag, consisting of a bracelet, brooch, and two sets of earrings, including lovely dangles. Author's collection. $425-525.

Two uniquely different brooch designs with matching earrings in cobalt blue and honeyed amber are laced with gold filigree balls and aurora borealis rhinestones. Courtesy of Debrah Mowat. $125-155.

Decadently rich Grand parure with massive collar necklace, five-link bracelet, tiered brooch and clip earrings. Deep burnt Sienna pear and tear drop rhinestones are heavily mounted with citrine aurora borealis chatons set in miniature frames that surround each stone. Lovely, lush, over the top. Courtesy of Linda Munn. $2500-3000.

Beautiful open back heliotrope keystones and iridescent aurora borealis rhinestones are layered throughout this beautiful tiered brooch, clip earrings and five-link bracelet demi-parure. Author's collection. $300-350.

Intense electric Capri blue demi-parure with large multi-dimensional leaf brooch and matching dangle earrings all highlighted with ice blue aurora borealis chatons. This set is so beautiful in person. Courtesy of Cleora Craw. $185-250.

Passionate Siam ruby red necklace and clip earrings demi-parure constructed in multiple layers with large open back Siam ruby red chatons dramatically constrasting with jet black navettes and floating ruby red rhinestone rosettes. Author's collection. Photo by Richard A. Stoner. $450-550.

Magnificent example of multi-dimensional construction beautifully displayed in this tiered brooch and clip earrings demi-parure. Layers of Montana blue and Capri blue rhinestones are laced with a multitude of ice blue aurora borealis chatons. Courtesy of Debrah Mowat. $225-300.

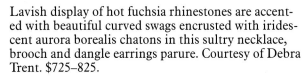

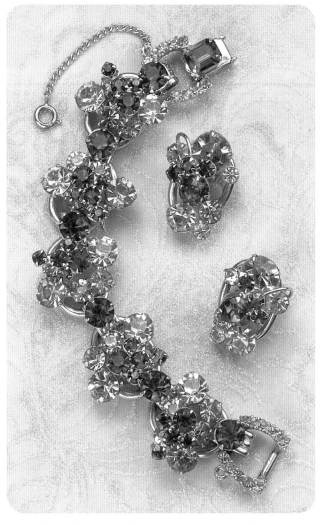

Lavish display of hot fuchsia rhinestones are accented with beautiful curved swags encrusted with iridescent aurora borealis chatons in this sultry necklace, brooch and dangle earrings parure. Courtesy of Debra Trent. $725–825.

Icy blue chatons are layered throughout this beautiful five-link bracelet and earrings demi-parure. The bracelet clasp is accented with a large Montana blue emerald cut rhinestone and ice blue chatons in a belt buckle style clasp. Each link is graced with a wire-over rhinestone in Montana blue. Author's collection. Photo by Richard A. Stoner. $175-200.

Look closely at the multiple colored rhinestones in the raised rosettes layered throughout this brooch. Highlights of deep Capri blue accentuate the bright pink chatons. Amethyst and pink rhinestones add the final touch. Courtesy of Debra Trent. $95-125.

Bejeweled display of open back navettes in ruby and emerald are accented by sapphire chatons that all highlight the rare deep sapphire diamond rhinestones in this incredible five-link bracelet and clip earrings demi-parure. Courtesy of Cleora Craw. $250-300.

Iridescent aurora borealis encrusted balls are the highlight in this brooch and earrings demi-parure accented with layers of hot pink and fuchsia rhinestones. Courtesy of Debra Trent. $135-155.

187

Tantalizing peridot Grand parure with necklace, five-link bracelet, brooch and three diverse sets of clip earrings. Beautiful teal blue rhinestones are blended in perfect harmony with olivine and iridescent aurora borealis chatons and raised rosette accents. Author's collection. $1300-1500.

Rich Montana blue pear shape rhinestones are layered throughout this chunky five-link bracelet and clip earrings demi-parure. The large iridescent aurora borealis rhinestones are the perfect accent to this delightful set. Courtesy of Cleora Craw. $175-200.

Warm and earthy cognac and citrine rhinestones are set in a beautiful leaf design with center gold filigree accents and tiny diamonté chatons in this autumn colored five-link bracelet and earrings ensemble. Courtesy of Debrah Mowat. $145-160.

Stunning gun-metal frosted glass rhinestones are mounted in various shapes and sizes in this dramatic five-link bracelet, tiered brooch and earrings demi-parure. Author's collection. Photo by Richard A. Stoner. $275-350.

A perfect example of how rich and luscious pieces look when combined together. This lovely necklace and brooch are layered with a kaleidoscope of colors ranging from peridot and fuchsia to burnt Sienna and hyacinth. Courtesy of Debra Trent. $75-225.

Romantically elegant necklace, five-link bracelet, pin-wheel brooch and dangle earrings parure with honey brown navettes and forest green marquis with peridot aurora borealis highlights. A fine example of how a few colors can have such an impact. Courtesy of Debrah Mowat. $675-775.

Enchanting combination of rhinestones in pink, blue, cognac, green and aquamarine with gold givré and banded marquis stones put a smile on your face in this brooch and earrings demi-parure with various prong supports. Author's collection. $95-125.

Lovely combination of Capri blue and pale blue against deep emerald green rhinestones makes such a statement. The open cut-work leaves are such a beautiful addition to the raised rosette accents in this sweet necklace. Courtesy of Debra Trent. $175-250.

Gorgeous necklace, five-link bracelet and clip earrings demi-parure is
layered with large Colorado topaz
chatons each framed with icy-green
aurora borealis beauties and hints of
cognac, olivine, peridot and hyacinth
rhinestones. Courtesy of Debra Trent.
$525-625.

Rare Châtelaine with iridescent aurora borealis rosettes
encircled with larger chatons with three cascading clear
rhinestone swags. Courtesy of Cleora Craw. $125-150.

Pale blue milk glass cushion cut stones
are highlighted with icy blue rhinestones
in this beautifully feminine five-link
bracelet and clip earrings demi-parure.
Author's collection. Photo by Richard A.
Stoner. $150-200.

191

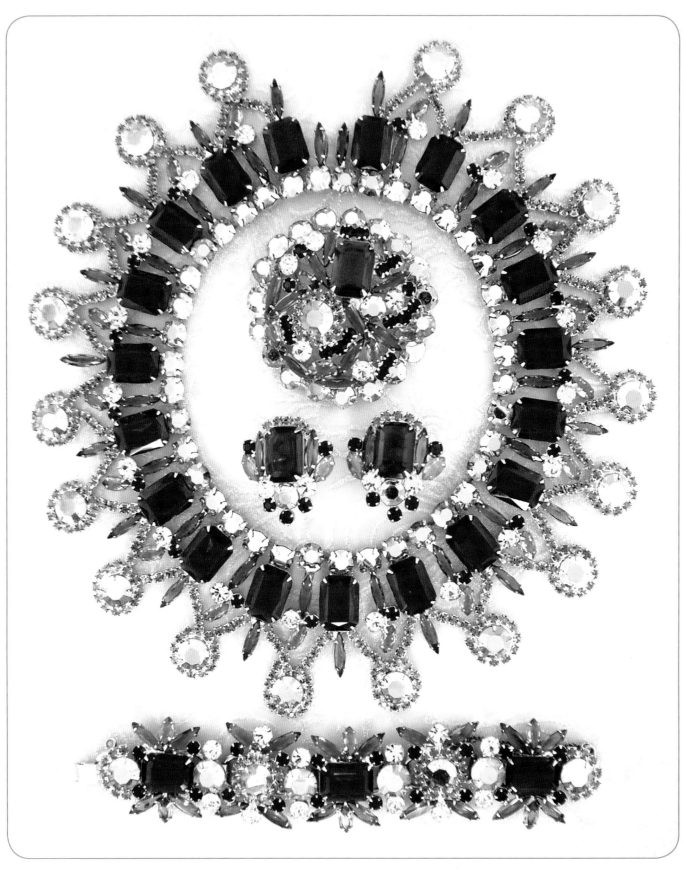

Lavish collar necklace with matching five-link bracelet, brooch and earrings is dressed with huge cushion cut octagon burnt amber open-back rhinestones combined with citrine, peridot, ruby red and jonquil accents in this incredible grand parure. Three sizes of champagne aurora borealis chatons add to this incomparable suite. Courtesy of Linda Munn. $2800-3500.

Radiant fuschia rhinestones are mounted in a fabulous dimensional design in this unique brooch and earrings demi-parure. The huge open back rhinestones are surrounded by two levels of aurora borealis chaton cages. Courtesy of Debra Trent. $225-275.

Dazzling hyacinth navettes are layered throughout this delightful floral brooch and earrings demi-parure. Use of multiple rhinestone wire-over accents are incorporated throughout each piece with iridescent aurora borelias chatons drawing attention to the huge cognac flower center. Courtesy of Debrah Mowat. $190-225.

Flowing leaf design brooch and earrings demi-parure layered with vivid chartreuse and hot fuchsia rhinestones is a perfect example of how two contrasting colors can really make a statement. Author's collection. $85-100.

Rich chocolate brown rhinestones dance with amber accents in this gorgeous necklace, five-link bracelet, tiered brooch and clip earrings parure. Champagne aurora borealis chatons are used in abundance to frame, highlight and add yet another element to this incredibly decadent suite. Courtesy of Debra Trent. $875-975.

Radiant brooch and clip earrings demi-parure covered with sizzling root-beer navettes and icy aurora borealis rhinestones are presented in a unique swirl pattern with raised rosette accents. Courtesy of Cleora Craw. $145-175.

Beautifully graceful design with an exquisite display of Bermuda blue, ice blue and teal blue rhinestones is built up in multi-dimensional layers in this beguiling necklace, five-link bracelet, brooch and clip earrings parure. Courtesy of Debra Trent. $900-975.

Sweet multi-dimensional brooch in fuchsia with articulated aurora borealis edging and a center flower accent. Courtesy of Debra Trent. $70-90.

Bright jonquil and hyacinth chatons are orchestrated in a dreamy design in this fabulous demi-parure complete with necklace, brooch and dangle earrings with icy aurora borealis highlights. Author's collection. Photo by Richard A. Stoner. $525-600.

Elaborate necklace, five-link bracelet, brooch and dangle earrings parure with an excellent example of multi-dimensional tiered construction. Deep emerald green, teal blue and iridescent aurora borealis rhinestones are built up in swedged sections offering a grand display of raised rosettes in various sizes. Courtesy of Debrah Mowat. $1100-1300.

I believe this set to be from the 1940's or early 1950's as it is one of the few that I have seen without the use of aurora borealis rhinestones. Flowing leaf brooch is paired with clip earrings in this elegant demi-parure with layers of Colorado topaz and amber open back navettes and jonquil chatons. Author's collection. Photo by Richard A. Stoner. $85-125.

Unique and beautiful deep cognac tapered keystone shards make a stunning statement in this five-link bracelet, necklace and brooch demi-parure. Note the interesting placement of the amber navettes and champagne aurora borealis chatons that draw attention to the dramatic keystones. Photo by Debrah Mowat. Courtesy of Lynn Compton. $575-625.

Dreamy brooch and earrings demi-parure set, in a whispy floral design incorporating deep Montana blue rhinestones with radiant vitreil aurora borealis chatons. Author's collection. $125-150.

Looking closely one will see that the table (top) of each deep amber kite rhinestone has a matt frosted finish, while the crown (side) is faceted with a brilliant luster. Touches of iridescent aurora borealis and pale cognac chatons are the finishing accents in this five-link bracelet and earrings demi-parure. Courtesy of Cleora Craw. $185-245.

The author performing, wearing the Juliana Sunburst parure. Private collection. Photo by Jennifer Gregory.

Well known "Sunburst" parure with rich Montana blue rhinestones displayed within what has become known as a Mayan theme. The elaborate necklace is embellished with cascades of icy aurora borealis chatons that are mimicked throughout the five-link bracelet, brooch and dangle earrings in this radiant parure. Author's collection. Photo by Richard A. Stoner. $750-850.

Bright hyacinth chatons are graced by chocolate brown baguettes, olivine navettes with Colorado topaz, warm Sienna and champagne rhinestones in this remarkable necklace, brooch and clip earrings demi-parure. Courtesy of Debra Trent. $425. - $500.

Absolutely mesmerizing brooch and dangle earrings demi-parure with deep fuchsia, rose pink and ballerina pink rhinestones. Note the double "caged" layers of vitreil aurora borealis chatons framed around each large fuchsia open back dangle. Courtesy of Cleora Craw. $250-325.

Illuminating icy blue rhinestones are mounted in dimensional layers throughout this enticing necklace, five-link bracelet, brooch and clip earrings parure. Iridescent aurora borealis encrusted balls and sweeping chaton laden horseshoes make this one elegant suite. Courtesy of Debra Trent. $950-1100.

Delicate flower brooch and earrings demi-parure encased with hyacinth, jonquil, champagne and light Colorado topaz rhinestones with a floating wire-over hyacinth flower displayed in the center of the brooch. Author's collection. Photo by Richard A. Stoner. $75-100.

Lovely display of burnt umber navettes against pale Colorado topaz rhinestones are beautifully set in a playful feather design in this necklace and earrings demi-parure. Courtesy of Debra Trent. $225-300.

Deep emerald green "Sunburst" necklace and tiered brooch demi-parure with iridescent melon aurora borealis highlights. Note the exceptional design in the complimentary spray brooch. Courtesy of Debrah Mowat. $325-425.

Fantastic emerald green oval rhinestones are elaborately framed with ice blue aurora borealis chatons and deep Capri blue marquis in this gorgeous five-link bracelet, dimensional brooch and clip earrings demi-parure. Courtesy of Cleora Craw. $275-300.

Multiple floral clusters are mounted between open back navettes in this delicate white milk glass brooch and earrings demi-parure. Author's collection. $65-80.

Incomparable cognac and Madiera rhinestone laden brooch, necklace and clip earrings demi-parure is many times referred to as the "owl" design. Note the elaborate use of double tiered aurora borealis rhinestone rosettes throughout this inimitable ensemble. Courtesy of Debra Trent. $750-850.

Another beautiful example of multi-dimensional construction is displayed in this brooch and clip earrings demi-parure laden with jonquil, olivine, peridot and cognac rhinestones with icy aurora borealis chatons. Courtesy of Debra Trent. $135-155.

Chunky Montana blue open back navettes are layered throughout this necklace and five-link bracelet demi-parure with iridescent blue aurora borealis chatons and raised rosette accents. Author's collection. Photograph by Richard A. Stoner. $325-425.

Delicate gold filigree leaves with diamonté accents are mounted over multiple levels of deep cognac navettes with rich citrine rhinestone accents in this five-link bracelet, brooch, and two contrasting pair of clip earrings demi-parure. Author's collection. $250-300.

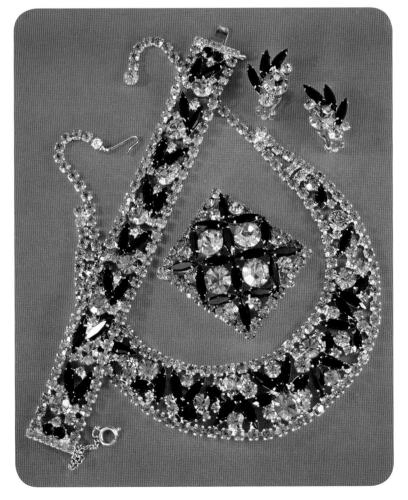

Fabulous jet black navettes are strategically placed throughout this bib necklace, flat back bracelet, brooch and clip earrings smoky gray rhinestone parure. Note the iridescent coating on the gray rhinestones that add to the drama of this set. Courtesy of Debra Trent. $550-600.

Smoky gray brooch and earrings demi-parure with another fine example of kite rhinestones that have a matt frosted finish on the table (top) with a shiny facted crown (side). Iridescent aurora borealis chatons and hints of gray rhinestones complete the ensemble. Courtesy of Cleora Craw. $150-200.

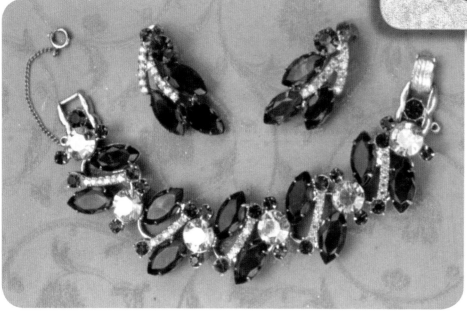

Bold Montana blue marquis are highlighted with champagne aurora borealis rhinestones in this fun five-link bracelet and clip earrings demi paure. Photo by Richard Stoner. $135-175.

Cascading Siam red navettes with multiple layers of ruby aurora borealis chatons are highlighted with raised rosette accents in this rare and dramatic dangle earrings and brooch demi-parure. Note the double layered rosettes throughout this suite. Courtesy of Debrah Mowat. $250-300.

Layers of rich burgundy and fuchsia navettes are positioned in a very dreamy theme in this gorgeous necklace, brooch and dangle earrings demi-parure. Courtesy of Debra Trent. $375-450.

Bright peridot matt and shiny marquis and navette rhinestones are highlighted with iridescent peridot aurora borealis chatons and emerald green accents in this bold brooch and earrings demi-parure. Author's collection. $75-95.

Sumptuous and fluid example of two color combination specialty rhinestones in this fabulous brooch, five-link bracelet, clamper bracelet and earrings parure mounted with watery pale citrine and banded amber open back rhinestones. Raised rosettes and icy white chatons finish of this dreamy ensemble. Notice – this set has also been found in green and blue. Courtesy of Cleora Craw. $415-500.

Deep Siam ruby red tiered brooch and clip earrings demi parure layered with contrasting red aurora borealis chatons with flashes of iridescent gold highlights. Author's collection. $110-125.

Rich jet black "Sunburst" necklace and tiered brooch demi-parure mounted with open back navettes and flashy iridescent aurora borealis accents in silvery smoke. Courtesy of Cleora Craw. $350-425.

Stunning matt red rhinestone dangle earrings measuring three inches in length. Author's collection. $75-100.

Warm chocolate frosted rhinestones are blended with bright Madeira chatons in this lovely tiered brooch. $75-95.

CHAPTER 17
Is It a Juliana?

It is not uncommon today to find a plethora of unsigned vintage costume jewelry on the market being sold as Juliana, when in fact, it is not. Many, many unsigned pieces of rhinestone costume jewelry were produced during the same period that Juliana style jewelry was manufactured. You will find unsigned pieces that are attributed to Weiss, Kramer, Schiaparelli, Schreiner, Kenneth Jay Lane, Trifari, Alice Caviness, Hobê, Mimi di N, and more. Thousands of pieces were created that incorporated the same cabochons, rhinestones, art glass, and cameos, but this does not qualify them as Juliana.

One must be armed with the knowledge and expertise to be able to make the right decision when purchasing DeLizza & Elster Juliana jewelry.

For example, if we study Weiss jewelry, we become familiar with the lovely rhinestone encrusted "crescent moon" shape that is layered throughout Weiss jewelry. Unsigned Weiss in this design is constantly being misrepresented as Juliana, when in fact, it is not. Other manufacturers also incorporated the "crescent moon" within their designs, but not DeLizza & Elster.

Unsigned beauty attributed to Weiss. Necklace and clip earrings demi-parure with example of rhinestone encrusted "crescent moon" design.

Another example are the beautiful pieces created by designer Anna DiMartino. Though most of her jewelry is also unsigned, many pieces arenow created with the "DiMartino Originals™" cartouche. While she uses many elements commonly found in DeLizza & Elster Juliana jewelry, the findings are completely different as well as the construction techniques. Her pieces are constantly being sold in online auctions as Juliana, commanding high prices, but upon close examination one will see that the design and components are quite unique and dissimilar.

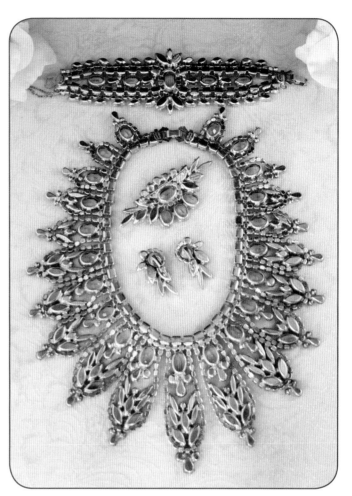

Anna DiMartino collar necklace, bracelet, brooch and clip earrings parure – Back view. Notice: Look closely at the necklace and bracelet clasps that are used by this artist as well as the oval cartouche featuring the "DiMartino Originals™" signature. Courtesy of Debra Trent.

Fabulous Anna DiMartino collar necklace, bracelet, brooch and clip earrings parure with spectacular show of rhinestones and art glass – Front view. Courtesy of Debra Trent.

In studying a Juliana Sunburst necklace the obvious clue is in counting the cascading drops. In viewing the photo one will see that there are seven cascading drops dangling off the center motif, whereas reproductions of this necklace have five cascading drops. Be aware of those traits that assist in establishing attribution and qualifying a piece as DeLizza & Elster Juliana jewelry. Observe the construction techniques, look closely at the stones that are incorporated in the piece as well as the style, findings and overall structure.

Juliana Sunburst necklace.

CHAPTER 18
A Juliana Mystery…Solved

Detail of the open dog tooth prongs and rhinestone mounting.

The lovely parure featured in this chapter has been frequently attributed to Schreiner. One can see how easy it would be to either cast this lovely suite aside with no attribution at all or call it an unsigned Schreiner. In viewing the prong support, we witness open dog-tooth prongs, which are a common element in Schreiner jewelry. (Hobê and Carnegie used these prongs, as well as many other companies). In reviewing the back structure of this set, note the fluted edges used in the metal construction throughout the assembly. This type of fluted edge is quite often incorporated in Schreiner jewelry and also referred to as "pie crust" edging. I have seen this exact necklace sold in online auctions as Schreiner, but here we are able to solve the "Juliana/Schreiner mystery" thanks to contributor Debrah Mowat. This is a perfect example of why the DeLizza & Elster five-link bracelets are such an important factor in establishing attribution. Without the matching five link bracelet one would never have guessed that this particular style of construction is attributed to DeLizza & Elster, thus confirming this lovely parure as a Juliana by DeLizza and Elster.

Detail of the fluted edges and construction assembly.

Aerial view of the construction assembly.

Front view of the
complete parure.

Detail of the five-link
bracelet.

Back view of the
five-link bracelet.

CHAPTER 19
Other Companies For Which
DeLizza & Elster Manufactured Jewelry

The photos displayed throughout this chapter make up a small selection of pieces from companies for which DeLizza & Elster manufactured jewelry. Examples of jewelry from Kramer, Kenneth Jay Lane, Weiss, Hattie Carnegie, Hobê, Celebrity, Accessocraft, Mimi di N, Sarah Coventry, and Madeleine give us an idea of how important DeLizza & Elster was for the booming costume jewelry era. Many of the examples represented reveal some very similar traits and elements that are often found in DeLizza & Elster Juliana jewelry as well.

Renata Tebaldi wearing Juliana and Kenneth Jay Lane jewelry. Private Collection.

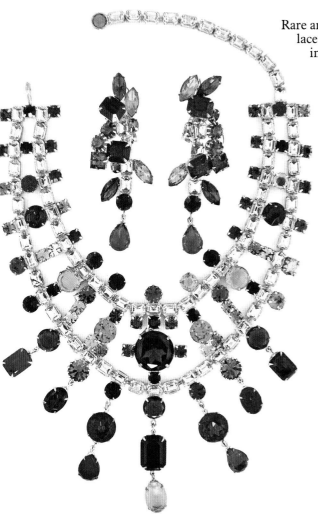

Rare and fabulous Kenneth Jay Lane "catwalk" necklace and dangle earrings demi-parure layered with an incredible array of aquamarine, cognac, Siam red, hyacinth, cognac, peridot, Capri blue, emerald green and fuchsia rhinestones in a mélange of shapes and sizes. Exquisite. Courtesy of Linda Munn. $2700–3500.

Beautiful Weiss japanned floral brooch with jet black center stone flanked by jet black open back navettes. $85-105.

Back view of Celebrity ensemble displaying the Celebrity signature in an oval cartouche. Courtesy of Debra Trent. $1400-1700.

Striking fuchsia navettes are elaborately combined with pale lilac and ballerina pink rhinestones with raised rosettes in this necklace, five-link bracelet, brooch and earrings parure by Celebrity. This is a well known design with various examples displayed throughout Chapter Sixteen. Courtesy of Debra Trent. $1400-1700.

Matt chatons in red, white and blue are mounted throughout this lovely brooch and clip earrings demi-parure by Kramer. $65-85.

Enchanting Sara Coventry brooch and dangle earrings demi-parure with original box. Peridot rhinestones are encased in gold filigree cups with peridot chaton accents. $75-125.

Unsigned piece attributed to Weiss. Massive brooch layered with icy clear rhinestones beautifully mounted in rhodium. $125-175.

Unsigned piece attributed to Weiss. Striking necklace mounted with a combination of deep purple and fuschia rhinetones are accented with delicate gold etched flowers with center sprays encompassing three faux pearls. Courtesy of Debra Trent. $150-200.

Dainty Celebrity gold carved roses clip earrings with clear rhinestone highlights. $25-45.

Gorgeous Hobê hand carved Cameo mesh bracelet and clip earrings demi-parure displaying deep amber, cognac, peridot and pale jonquil rhinestones. Notice the mesh fringe near the clasp so perfectly reminiscent of the Victorian era. Courtesy of Debrah Mowat. $350-450.

Sumptuous Kenneth Jay Lane run-way necklace and bracelet demi-parure with intense colors of Siam red, emerald green, hot pink, heliotrope, cognac, hyacinth, teal blue, jonquil, purple, champagne and black rhinestones layered in a very unique and extraordinarily contemporary design. Courtesy of Linda Munn. $2500-3000.

Unsigned beauty attributed to Weiss. Intense peacock volcano art glass cabochons with heliotrope, silver, amethyst and lavendar veining are the highlight in this knock-out necklace and clip earrings demi-parure. Note: Schiaparelli pieces have also been found with these art glass cabochons. $225-275.

Unsigned piece attributed to Elsa Schiaparelli. Fantastic peacock watermelon stones are flanked by watery open back aquamarine and ice blue rhinestones with aurora borealis highlights in this dreamy brooch and clip earrings demi-parure. Notice: This set is always attributed to Juliana in on-line auctions. Photo by Richard A. Stoner. $150-250.

Delicate Hobê brooch is layered with opaque turquoise and milk glass raised rosettes set in gold gilded cages with the formidable "rolled heart" design, so often used by DeLizza and Elster. $75-150.

Large and intricately detailed Weiss butterfly brooch mounted with a profusion of rhinestones resembling cutwork lace. Courtesy of Debra Trent. $125-150.

Delicious Kramer brooch and earrings demi-parure mounted with layers of chaton encrusted floating crescent moons surrounded by Ruby red, topaz, cognac and olivine rhinestones with a touch of facted aurora borealis dangles. Courtesy of Debra Trent. $110-150.

Multi-colored Kenneth Jay Lane brooch with original hang-tag set with a flamboyant display of open back rhinestones. $100-150.

Show stopping rare Mimi di N (Mimi di Nescemi) massive bib necklace with multiple cascading drops of large open back emerald green tear drop rhinestones smothered in icy white chatons. Courtesy of Linda Munn. $1300-1500.

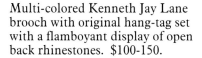

Unsigned piece attributed to Madeleine. Pale iridescent butterscotch cushion cut stones are the focal point in this necklace, bracelet and clip earrings ensemble with deep amber and pale jonquil accents. Courtesy of Debra Trent. $225-275.

Inticing pastel color rhinestones are the focal point in this densely structured ultra-feminine Kenneth Jay Lane collar necklace. Courtesy of Linda Munn. $850-1000.

Famous Sarah Coventry "Blue Lagoon" demi-parure with brooch and earrings on original factory cards. Note the multi-dimensional layering of rhinestones throughout this well known suite. $75-125.

Multiple sizes of iridescent aurora borealis rhinestones are mounted in various levels highlighting each center rosette in these lovely Weiss earrings. $45-65.

Collection of Mimi di N (Mimi di Nescemi) belt buckles. $55-75 each.

Graceful Hattie Carnegie swan figural brooch with faux turquoise beads mounted into the body. $110-140.

The polished mother-of-pearl back is the focal point in this sweet Kenneth Jay Lane turtle brooch with glistening rhinestone head and eyes. $75-100.

Deep cobalt blue Kramer clip earrings with pave set rhinestone accents. $25-35.

Bold and heavy Accessocraft necklace inlaid with faux carnelian, jade, tiger eye and onyx cabochons. The large center pendant measures a wopping seven inches in length by five inches wide. $125-175.

Succulent Kenneth Jay Lane apricot brooch is mounted with deep cognac and Madeira rhinestones, baguette stem and faux jade leaves. $75-95.

Scintilating Kenneth Jay Lane massive bib necklace, clamper bracelet, brooch and clip earrings parure with a grand display of rivoli, margarita and tourmaline watermelon rhinestones laced with accents of hyacinth, emerald green, Madeira and burnt tangerine chatons. Photo by Don Friedman. Courtesy of Terri Friedman. $2300-2700.

CHAPTER 20
Repair and Restoration

When considering repairing and/or restoring a piece of Juliana jewelry, it seems that no limits or boundaries exist. Often a piece is purchased because it is rare or highly desirable or it is the one last piece needed to complete an ensemble. If the condition of the piece warrants restoration the challenge will be in finding the right person to handle the task. In determining how far to go in the repair and restoration process it really comes down to a few factors: how bad do you need the piece, how rare is the piece, what kind of condition is it in and what extent are you willing to take in bringing it back to its original glory?

Most of the time repairs like replacing a rhinestone, adding dangles or straightening a pin back can be simply handled. Other circumstances require the use of a professional. I have witnessed fabulous pieces of Juliana where wire supports have been clipped off to remove dangles, stones have been replaced with stones of an inferior color and bracelet links have been removed to shorten a five link bracelet. In this case it is imperative that great length be taken in researching a first class costume jewelry repair and restoration expert. It is important to ask for a quote right from the beginning. Be very explicit regarding your repairs. Ask for recommendations as well as soldering techniques and how the solder will be concealed if the item being repaired is gold metal. Many times gold paint is applied over the solder to cover the silver solder, which is not permanent and will rub off quickly. Be specific about findings. If you are missing a connecting link to a Juliana Bracelet, make sure you specifically request that the added link match the other links exactly.

In my experience, I have found that it is particularly important to ask that one pair of hands be used in the repair or restoration process. For example, if you are in need of having dangles replaced that have been removed, make sure that one person handles the turning of the head-pins for those dangles or they will all come out in various sizes and lengths. This applies to rhinestone mounting as well as soldering. Ask that one pair of hands handle each task so that the final outcome is consistent.

In an interview with Matthew Ribarich, of "Vintage Costume Jewelry Stone Replacement & Repair," he communicated the importance of understanding the repair and restoration process. With thirty years of experience to his credit, he stresses the necessity of learning the process of good quality repairs and restoration, which will take time, patience, and money. If you are going to work at this process on your own, Mr. Ribarich states, "Having the correct tools and stones will assist you and make your job easier and your finished product professional looking. When starting, you will need the basic tools which include Millimeter Gauges, Ball burr's, Hypo Glue, Dopsticks (used to pick up stones), plastic bags for storing your stones as well as a collection of rhinestones. Bending prongs to remove rhinestones takes experience and one should attempt this daunting task after practicing on broken or discarded jewelry first."

Mr. Ribarich stocks over six million vintage stones from the 1930s to the 1980s, with close to a hundred colors to choose from. He also carries one of the largest inventories of Swarovski rhinestones, as well as many of the tools required to restore vintage costume jewelry. He works with over 5,000 clients each year and his expert restoration skills were used in the movie "Notebook."

CHAPTER 21
Storage and Care

When costume jewelry was first manufactured, it was meant to be worn during a season or two and then tossed aside, never to be used again. It is surprising to see how wonderful these beautiful examples from the past have held up over time. With proper care and storage, these pieces will keep all the sparkle and shine they had when they were first produced.

Many collectors have specific ideas regarding the storage of their Juliana to the extent of keeping them in safety deposit boxes as well as home safes. Some collectors display their pieces as if they were in a Museum. Ideally pieces should be stored in a manner that protects them from the elements, namely light, dust and moisture, which causes metal deterioration (oxidation).

I have adopted a storage system that contributor Debrah Mowat introduced to me that is not only cost effective, but very efficient in protecting my collection while allowing me the ability to view pieces without much handling. Simple photo display boxes or memory boxes work wonderfully in protecting pieces, keeping them free from dust, while still allowing easy access. Pieces are beautifully displayed and admired through the glass top and stacked neatly one on top of the other, resembling a lovely jewelry armoire. The final precautionary tool is the addition of a few packets of silica gel layered in the corners of the boxes to protect against moisture.

Example of a storage display photo box with a collection of Juliana jewelry. Courtesy of Debrah Mowat.

Example of a storage display box with upper level removed, to view two levels of a Juliana jewelry collection. Courtesy of Debrah Mowat

Resources

CLEORA'S VINTAGE COSTUME JEWELRY
Contact: Cleora Craw
104 County Rd.108
Burnet, TX 78611
Phone: 512-756-2408
cleora78611@yahoo.com or
Specializing in: DeLizza & Elster Juliana and Vintage costume jewelry
Member of: ★Discovering Juliana Jewelry (DJJ)

JENNIFER GREGORY
PreciousCPhoto@aol.com
Specializing in: Photo restoration, photography

DEBRAH MOWAT
AMAZING FACETS - Rubylane Shop
Contact: Debrah Mowat
Ontario, Canada
www.rubylane.com/shops/amazingfacets
Specializing in: DeLizza & Elster Juliana
Member of: ★Discovering Juliana Jewelry (DJJ)

LINDA MUNN
Munn & Associates
Longview, TX
903-399-6167
ljmunn@cablelynx.com
Private collector buying and selling as Ljools on EBAY
Specializing in DeLizza & Elster Juliana, Schiaparelli and all the GOOD BIG stuff !
Member of: ★Discovering Juliana Jewelry (DJJ)

MATTHEW RIBARICH
Mrstones4u@aol.com
www.mrstones.com
757-558-9997 Phone & Fax
757-558-8151 Phone & Fax
Vintage Costume Jewelry Stone replacement, restoration & repair

RHUMBA!
Terri Friedman
PO Box 148186
Chicago, IL 60604
www.tace.com/rhumba
adon13@aol.com
Phone: 773-929-9007
Fax: 773-525-1920
Specializing in: Quality Vintage Designer & Contemporary Costume Jewelry, Silver, Bakelite & Estate Jewelry
Member of: Jewel Collect, Jewelry Ring, ★Discovering Juliana Jewelry (DJJ)

DEBRA TRENT
Deb's Vintage Costume Jewelry on Rubylane
www.rubylane.com/shops/debsvintage
www.debsvintagecostumejewelry.com
Specializing in: DeLizza & Elster Juliana, Regency, and quality vintage jewelry

★DISCOVERING JULIANA JEWELRY (DJJ)
http://groups.com/group/discoveringjulianajewelry/join

Glossary

The terminology incorporated within this glossary reflects the unique language that is used among Juliana aficionados that has become standardized in the costume jewelry industry. It represents how this jewelry is defined among collectors. Many of the terms are also used when addressing costume and fine jewelry in general.

Art Deco - Jewelry that incorporates modern, stylized, triangular and geometric lines reflecting the Art Deco period.

art glass - Fancy stones that are either painted, molded, stippled, pressed, filled with copper or gold or embedded with foil to achieve a faux look often times resembling the real thing.

Aurora Borealis - Invented in 1953, an iridescent coating that is applied to a rhinestone that gives it a luminous glow filled with multiple colors when refracted by light.

baguette - A rectangular-cut rhinestone, usually narrow with four pointed corners.

bail - A small hook or loop attached to the back of a brooch that enables the brooch to also be worn as a necklace when a chain is suspended through the bail.

bar-pin - A rectangular piece of hardware with a pin attached to it that is soldered to the back of a brooch/pin.

box and tongue clasp – A square box at one end with an opening that secures the tongue from the other end that enters the clasp. These are found on DeLizza & Elster flat-back bracelets.

brass leaves - Delicate etched gilded gold leaves that are swedged into the bottom of a piece of jewelry and layered over the top to create a lovely dimensional look found in DeLizza & Elster jewelry.

cabochon - An oval or round domed shaped smooth stone without facets and a flat back.

cameo - A carved design created from above or on top of a surface of glass, shell, plastic or other material.

camphor glass - A frosted, cloudy glass resembling quartz crystal that is molded or pressed into a desired shape, usually with a center diamonté accent.

Carmen Miranda design - A design incorporating colorful seed pods that are reminiscent of the dangling fruit that the actress Carmen Miranda was known for.

cat's eye - A specialty glass cabochon infused with multiple colors of foil and glass creating a look that resembles the iridescent glow of cat's eyes.

châtelaine - Two pins that are connected by draping rhinestones that could be attached to both sides of a collar to keep a sweater, cape or light jacket in place.

chaton - A round faceted rhinestone usually with eight facets.

citrine - A semi-precious stone ranging from a pale yellow to bright yellow color.

clamper bracelet - A bracelet that is open and closed by a spring loaded clamp.

cushion cut - A stone bearing delicate rounded edges rather than sharp cut edges.

D&E - Abbreviation used for DeLizza and Elster.

demi-parure - A matching set of jewelry that includes two or three pieces all within the same design and theme.

diamanté - A faceted glass or crystal stone also referred to as a rhinestone.

domed construction - An assemblage of metal components that are joined together on top of one another, providing a curved appearance resembling a dome.

Easter egg cabochon - A man-made stone that has been painted and decorated with multiple colors that seems to resemble Easter eggs.

etched glass - Various shapes and themes are carved into glass to create a design.

faux - In reference to costume jewelry, an imitation or artificial stone or mineral that is fabricated to look like a real stone or mineral.

figural brooch - Those designs which represent birds, butterflies, turtles and other animals as well as objects such as instruments and people.

filigree - Cut open-work designs applied to metal that represents fine lace or batting.

findings - Metal pieces that are used to connect and support jewelry such as clasps, hooks, links, pins, chains, etc.

five-link construction - Five links that are joined together by metal connectors that are typically inlaid with rhinestones and art glass and used in DeLizza & Elster bracelets and necklaces.

givré - An art glass stone that has two or more colors swirled throughout for a marbled effect. DeLizza & Elster givré stones have been found in emerald green, warm brown, sapphire blue, amethyst, fuchsia and a golden yellow.

gold or copper fluss - A copper ore that is melted into glass that creates a coppery speckled or banded effect throughout the stone.

grand parure - A matching set of jewelry that includes necklace, bracelet, brooch and earrings plus one or more extra piece that brings the complete ensemble to more than four pieces.

gun metal - Deep gray color found on findings which is a colored coating that is applied to the metal.

head pin - A wire finding that is used to suspend and secure a dangle.

intaglio - A carved design created from underneath or behind the surface of a piece of glass, shell, ivory or other material.

iridescent - Various hues of colors that change when refracted by light or when seen from different angles.

J-hook - The catch used to secure a necklace off of a rhinestone chain, also referred to as a shepherd's hook.

Japanned - Deep black color found on findings which is actually a coating that is applied to the metal.

joint and catch pin assembly - A finding with a long wire with a pointed tip that catches under a mechanism that locks the wire (catch) with the other end being the hinged area that releases the wire to secure a brooch.

keystone - A rectangular rhinestone that is tapered at one end and resembles the open area in which a key would be used to open an older style door lock.

kite stone - A rhinestone that is shaped like a kite.

margarita - A specialty rhinestone that has a raised center with a scalloped edge that runs all the way around the stone. The center is usually mounted and secured with a center rhinestone.

marquis - A rhinestone that is oval shaped with pointed ends, also referred to as a navette.

melted solder mounds - Small raised mounds created by solder being melted into the construction assembly process which can be viewed on the back of DeLizza & Elster pieces.

marriage - A term used in the costume jewelry industry referring to the union of two or more dissimilar pieces of jewelry that do not have the same consistent theme throughout each piece.

millefiori - A technique which involves the melting of multiple colors of glass into a long glass rod using a torch. While still warm the glass is sliced to reveal a floral pattern. Millefiori means "one thousand flowers" in Italian.

molded glass - Glass that has been imprinted with a design which is achieved by pouring hot glass into a mold to create the desired design.

navette - An elongated oval shaped stone with tapered, pointed ends.

open-back setting - A setting within a mounting which allows both foiled and unfoiled rhinestones and cabochons to be viewed from the back.

openwork - Metal that has been cut out in areas that somewhat resembles lace.

parure - A matching set of four pieces of jewelry that includes necklace, bracelet, brooch and earrings all within the same design and theme.

paste-set rhinestones - Rhinestones that are mounted with glue rather than prongs.

pressed glass - Glass that is impressed with a mold to create a design that many times resembles hand etching.

prong - Metal supports that are used as mountings to support rhinestones, cabochons and other stones.

rhinestone - A highly faceted glass stone created to imitate diamonds and fine stones like rubies, emeralds and sapphires available in all shapes and sizes with foiled or unfoiled backs.

rhinestone chain - A long chain of rhinestones connected to one another with a very short piece of metal. An example would be the rhinestone laden chains running off of DeLizza & Elster necklaces.

rhodium - A silvery gray metal from the platinum family used to plate costume jewelry.

rivoli - A highly faceted rhinestone that is pointed at the top. The colors are mesmerizing and often refract many colors of a rainbow.

rivet or **eyelet** - A small circular piece of hardware used to secure and join multiple pieces together.

rosettes - One large center rhinestone flanked by a circling of smaller rhinestones resembling a flower.

safety chain - A short chain that is attached to both sides of a bracelet clasp with a spring ring finding on one end.

saphiret glass - A specialty stone that incorporates minute quantities of gold into sapphire colored glass resulting in a warm cappuccino color with pink and pale blue highlights.

shepherd's hook - A hook that is soldered to the end of a rhinestone chain to secure a necklace, also referred to as a J Hook.

skip-chain - A strip of metal used to secure two pieces of metal together to create a design.

stippling (**stippled relief**) - A technique that creates an uneven surface by using certain tools to mark the surface. Addition of paint applied in a pointy and layered manner gives a dimensional look to the surface as viewed in the DeLizza & Elster Easter egg cabochons.

suite - A matched set of jewelry consisting of three or more pieces.

swedging - The use of a rivet or eyelet to secure and join multiple pieces together.

tiered construction - Multiple layers or rows joined one upon another to create a multi-dimensional look.

tiger eye - A specialty stone with brown marble veining running through a deep citrine base.

vitreil - A luminous coating applied to rhinestones that give off a multi-lustrous shower of colors.

watermelon tourmaline - A natural mineral with banded stripes of colors running through it that vary in color from pale citrine to pink to green. In costume jewelry watermelon rhinestones mimic the colors of natural watermelon tourmaline.

wire-over (floating suspended wire) - A piece of wire that is joined from behind a piece of jewelry and then suspended over the front to display a layer of rhinestones, creating another element of dimension.

Bibliography

Bell, Jeanenne. *Answers to Questions About Old Jewelry*. Iola, Wisconsin: Krause Publications, 2003.

Carroll, Julia C. *Costume Jewelry 101*. Paducah, Kentucky: Collectors Books, 2004.

_____. *Costume Jewelry 202*. Paducah, Kentucky: Collectors Books, 2007.

Romero, Christie. *Warman's Jewelry Identification and Price Guide*. Iola, Wisconsin: Krause Publications, 2002.

Schiffer, Nancy. *Rhinestones!* Atglen, Pennsylvania: Schiffer Publishing, Ltd., 2001

The curtain call, as the author performs while wearing the red Aurora Borealis parure. Private collection. Photo by Jennifer Gregory.